CONGO

CONGO

EXPLORATION, REFORM, AND A BRUTAL LEGACY

BRUCE AND BECKY DUROST~FISH

INTRODUCTORY ESSAY BY
Dr. Richard E. Leakey
Chairman, Wildlife Clubs
of Kenya Association
⁓✟⁓
AFTERWORD BY
Deirdre Shields

CHELSEA HOUSE PUBLISHERS
Philadelphia
In association with Covos Day Books, South Africa

CHELSEA HOUSE PUBLISHERS

EDITOR IN CHIEF Sally Cheney
PRODUCTION MANAGER Pamela Loos
ART DIRECTOR Sara Davis
PICTURE EDITOR Judy L. Hasday
MANAGING EDITOR James D. Gallagher
SENIOR PRODUCTION EDITOR LeeAnne Gelletly
ASSOCIATE ART DIRECTOR Takeshi Takahashi
SERIES DESIGNER Keith Trego
COVER DESIGN Emiliano Begnardi

The Chelsea House World Wide Web address is http://www.chelseahouse.com

First Printing
1 3 5 7 9 8 6 4 2
Library of Congress Cataloging-in-Publication Data

Fish, Bruce.
    The Congo / Bruce & Becky Durost Fish.
        p. cm. — (Exploration of Africa)
    Includes bibliographical references and index.
    ISBN 0-7910-6198-1 (alk. paper)
    1. Congo River Valley—Discovery and exploration—Juvenile literature 2. Africa,
Central—Discovery and exploration—Juvenile literature. 3. Congo (Democratic
Republic)—Discovery and exploration—Juvenile literature. 4. Stanley, Henry
M. (Henry Morton), 1841–1904—Juvenile literature. 5. Explorers—Africa,
Sub-Saharan—Biography—Juvenile literature. 6. Explorers—Great Britain—
Biography—Juvenile literature. [1. Congo River Valley—Discovery and explo-
ration. 2. Congo (Democratic Republic) 3. Stanley, Henry M. (Henry Morton),
1841–1904. 4. Explorers.] I. Fish, Becky Durost. II. Title. III. Exploration of
Africa, the emerging nations.

DT639 .F57 2000
967.51'01—dc21

                                                            00-055591

The photographs in this book are from the Royal Geographical Society Picture Library. Most are being published for the first time.

The Royal Geographical Society Picture Library provides an unrivaled source of over half a million images of
peoples and landscapes from around the globe. Photographs date from the 1840s onwards on a variety of subjects including the British Colonial Empire, deserts, exploration, indigenous peoples, landscapes, remote desti-
nations, and travel.

Photography, beginning with the daguerreotype in 1839, is only marginally younger than the Society, which
encouraged its explorers to use the new medium from its earliest days. From the remarkable mid-19th century
black-and-white photographs to color transparencies of the late 20th century, the focus of the collection is not the
generic stock shot but the portrayal of man's resilience, adaptability, and mobility in remote parts of the world.

In organizing this project, we have incurred many debts of gratitude. Our first, though, is to the professional staff
of the Picture Library for their generous assistance, especially to Joanna Scadden, Picture Library Manager.

CONTENTS

Exploration of Africa: The Emerging Nations

THE DARK CONTINENT

DR. RICHARD E. LEAKEY

THE CONCEPT OF AFRICAN exploration has been greatly influenced by the hero status given to the European adventurers and missionaries who went off to Africa in the last century. Their travels and travails were certainly extraordinary and nobody can help but be impressed by the tremendous physical and intellectual courage that was so much a characteristic of people such as Livingstone, Stanley, Speke, and Baker, to name just a few. The challenges and rewards that Africa offered, both in terms of commerce and also "saved souls," inspired people to take incredible risks and endure personal suffering to a degree that was probably unique to the exploration of Africa.

I myself was fortunate enough to have had the opportunity to organize one or two minor expeditions to remote spots in Africa where there were no roads or airfields and marching with porters and/or camels was the best option at the time. I have also had the thrill of being with people untouched and often unmoved by contact with Western or other technologically based cultures, and these experiences remain for me amongst the most exciting and salutary of my life. With the contemporary revolution in technology, there will be few if any such opportunities again. Indeed I often find myself slightly saddened by the realization that were life ever discovered on another planet, exploration would doubtless be done by remote sensing and making full use of artificial, digital intelligence. At least it is unlikely to be in my lifetime and this is a relief!

INTRODUCTION

Notwithstanding all of this, I believe that the age of exploration and discovery in Africa is far from over. The future offers incredible opportunities for new discoveries that will push back the frontiers of knowledge. This endeavor will of course not involve exotic and arduous journeys into malaria-infested tropical swamps, but it will certainly require dedication, team work, public support, and a conviction that the rewards to be gained will more than justify the efforts and investment.

EARLY EXPLORERS

Many of us were raised and educated at school with the belief that Africa, the so-called Dark Continent, was actually discovered by early European travelers and explorers. The date of this "discovery" is difficult to establish, and anyway a distinction has always had to be drawn between northern Africa and the vast area south of the Sahara. The Romans certainly had information about the continent's interior as did others such as the Greeks. A diverse range of traders ventured down both the west coast and the east coast from at least the ninth century, and by the tenth century Islam had taken root in a number of new towns and settlements established by Persian and Arab interests along the eastern tropical shores. Trans-African trade was probably under way well before this time, perhaps partly stimulated by external interests.

Close to the beginning of the first millennium, early Christians were establishing the Coptic church in the ancient kingdom of Ethiopia and at other coastal settlements along Africa's northern Mediterranean coast. Along the west coast of Africa, European trade in gold, ivory, and people was well established by the sixteenth century. Several hundred years later, early in the 19th century, the systematic penetration and geographical exploration of Africa was undertaken by Europeans seeking geographical knowledge and territory and looking for opportunities not only for commerce but for the chance to spread the Gospel. The extraordinary narratives of some of the journeys of early European travelers and adventurers in Africa are a vivid reminder of just how recently Africa has become embroiled in the power struggles and vested interests of non-Africans.

THE DARK CONTINENT

AFRICA'S GIFT TO THE WORLD

My own preoccupation over the past thirty years has been to study human prehistory, and from this perspective it is very clear that Africa was never "discovered" in the sense in which so many people have been and, perhaps, still are being taught. Rather, it was Africans themselves who found that there was a world beyond their shores.

Prior to about two million years ago, the only humans or proto-humans in existence were confined to Africa; as yet, the remaining world had not been exposed to this strange mammalian species, which in time came to dominate the entire planet. It is no trivial matter to recognize the cultural implications that arise from this entirely different perspective of Africa and its relationship to the rest of humanity.

How many of the world's population grow up knowing that it was in fact African people who first moved and settled in southern Europe and Central Asia and migrated to the Far East? How many know that Africa's principal contribution to the world is in fact humanity itself? These concepts are quite different from the notion that Africa was only "discovered" in the past few hundred years and will surely change the commonly held idea that somehow Africa is a "laggard," late to come onto the world stage.

It could be argued that our early human forebears—the *Homo erectus* who moved out of Africa—have little or no bearing on the contemporary world and its problems. I disagree and believe that the often pejorative thoughts that are associated with the Dark Continent and dark skins, as well as with the general sense that Africans are somehow outside the mainstream of human achievement, would be entirely negated by the full acceptance of a universal African heritage for all of humanity. This, after all, is the truth that has now been firmly established by scientific inquiry.

The study of human origins and prehistory will surely continue to be important in a number of regions of Africa and this research must continue to rank high on the list of relevant ongoing exploration and discovery. There is still much to be learned about the early stages of human development, and the age of the "first humans"—the first bipedal apes—has not been firmly established. The current hypothesis is that prior to five million years ago there were no bipeds, and this

INTRODUCTION

would mean that humankind is only five million years old. Beyond Africa, there were no humans until just two million years ago, and this is a consideration that political leaders and people as a whole need to bear in mind.

RECENT HISTORY

When it comes to the relatively recent history of Africa's contemporary people, there is still considerable ignorance. The evidence suggests that there were major migrations of people within the continent during the past 5,000 years, and the impact of the introduction of domestic stock must have been quite considerable on the way of life of many of Africa's people. Early settlements and the beginnings of nation states are, as yet, poorly researched and recorded. Although archaeological studies have been undertaken in Africa for well over a hundred years, there remain more questions than answers.

One question of universal interest concerns the origin and inspiration for the civilization of early Egypt. The Nile has, of course, offered opportunities for contacts between the heart of Africa and the Mediterranean seacoast, but very little is known about human settlement and civilization in the upper reaches of the Blue and White Nile between 4,000 and 10,000 years ago. We do know that the present Sahara Desert is only about 10,000 years old; before this Central Africa was wetter and more fertile, and research findings have shown that it was only during the past 10,000 years that Lake Turkana in the northern Kenya was isolated from the Nile system. When connected, it would have been an excellent connection between the heartland of the continent and the Mediterranean.

Another question focuses on the extensive stone-walled villages and towns in Southern Africa. The Great Zimbabwe is but one of thousands of standing monuments in East, Central, and Southern Africa that attest to considerable human endeavor in Africa long before contact with Europe or Arabia. The Neolithic period and Iron Age still offer very great opportunities for exploration and discovery.

As an example of the importance of history, let us look at the modern South Africa where a visitor might still be struck by the not-too-subtle representation of a past that, until a few years ago, only "began" with the arrival of Dutch settlers some 400 years back. There are, of course, many pre-Dutch sites, including extensive fortified towns where kingdoms and nation states had thrived hundreds of years before contact with Europe; but this evidence has been poorly documented and even more poorly portrayed.

Few need to be reminded of the sparseness of Africa's precolonial written history. There are countless cultures and historical narratives that have been recorded only as oral history and legend. As postcolonial Africa further consolidates itself, history must be reviewed and deepened to incorporate the realities of precolonial human settlement as well as foreign contact. Africa's identity and self-respect is closely linked to this.

One of the great tragedies is that African history was of little interest to the early European travelers who were in a hurry and had no brief to document the details of the people they came across during their travels. In the basements of countless European museums, there are stacked shelves of African "curios"—objects taken from the people but seldom documented in terms of the objects' use, customs, and history.

There is surely an opportunity here for contemporary scholars to do something. While much of Africa's precolonial past has been obscured by the slave trade, colonialism, evangelism, and modernization, there remains an opportunity, at least in some parts of the continent, to record what still exists. This has to be one of the most vital frontiers for African exploration and discovery as we approach the end of this millennium. Some of the work will require trips to the field, but great gains could be achieved by a systematic and coordinated effort to record the inventories of European museums and archives. The Royal Geographical Society could well play a leading role in this chapter of African exploration. The compilation of a central data bank on what is known and what exists would, if based on a coordinated initiative to record the customs and social organization of Africa's remaining indigenous peoples, be a huge contribution to the heritage of humankind.

Medicines and Foods

On the African continent itself, there remain countless other areas for exploration and discovery. Such endeavors will be achieved without the fanfare of great expeditions and high adventure as was the case during the last century and they should, as far as possible, involve

INTRODUCTION

exploration and discovery of African frontiers by Africans themselves. These frontiers are not geographic: they are boundaries of knowledge in the sphere of Africa's home-grown cultures and natural world.

Indigenous knowledge is a very poorly documented subject in many parts of the world, and Africa is a prime example of a continent where centuries of accumulated local knowledge is rapidly disappearing in the face of modernization. I believe, for example, that there is much to be learned about the use of wild African plants for both medicinal and nutritional purposes. Such knowledge, kept to a large extent as the experience and memory of elders in various indigenous communities, could potentially have far-reaching benefits for Africa and for humanity as a whole.

The importance of new remedies based on age-old medicines cannot be underestimated. Over the past two decades, international companies have begun to take note and to exploit certain African plants for pharmacological preparations. All too often, Africa has not been the beneficiary of these "discoveries," which are, in most instances, nothing more than the refinement and improvement of traditional African medicine. The opportunities for exploration and discovery in this area are immense and will have assured economic return on investment. One can only hope that such work will be in partnership with the people of Africa and not at the expense of the continent's best interests.

Within the same context, there is much to be learned about the traditional knowledge of the thousands of plants that have been utilized by different African communities for food. The contemporary world has become almost entirely dependent, in terms of staple foods, on the cultivation of only six principal plants: corn, wheat, rice, yams, potatoes, and bananas. This cannot be a secure basis to guarantee the food requirements of more than five billion people.

Many traditional food plants in Africa are drought resistant and might well offer new alternatives for large-scale agricultural development in the years to come. Crucial to this development is finding out what African people used before exotics were introduced. In some rural areas of the continent, it is still possible to learn about much of this by talking to the older generation. It is certainly a great shame that some of the early European travelers in Africa were ill equipped to study and record details of diet and traditional plant use, but I am sure that, although it is late, it is not too late. The compilation of a pan-African database on what is known about the use of the continent's plant resources is a vital matter requiring action.

VANISHING SPECIES

In the same spirit, there is as yet a very incomplete inventory of the continent's other species. The inevitable trend of bringing land into productive management is resulting in the loss of unknown but undoubtedly large numbers of species. This genetic resource may be invaluable to the future of Africa and indeed humankind, and there really is a need for coordinated efforts to record and understand the continent's biodiversity.

In recent years important advances have been made in the study of tropical ecosystems in Central and South America, and I am sure that similar endeavors in Africa would be rewarding. At present, Africa's semi-arid and highland ecosystems are better understood than the more diverse and complex lowland forests, which are themselves under particular threat from loggers and farmers. The challenges of exploring the biodiversity of the upper canopy in the tropical forests, using the same techniques that are now used in Central American forests, are fantastic and might also lead to eco-tourist developments for these areas in the future.

It is indeed an irony that huge amounts of money are being spent by the advanced nations in an effort to discover life beyond our own planet, while at the same time nobody on this planet knows the extent and variety of life here at home. The tropics are especially relevant in this regard and one can only hope that Africa will become the focus of renewed efforts of research on biodiversity and tropical ecology.

AN AFROCENTRIC VIEW

Overall, the history of Africa has been presented from an entirely Eurocentric or even Caucasocentric perspective, and until recently this has not been adequately reviewed. The penetration of Africa, especially during the last century, was important in its own way; but today the realities of African history, art, culture, and politics are better known. The time has come to regard African history in terms of what has happened in Africa itself, rather than simply in terms of what non-African individuals did when they first traveled to the continent.

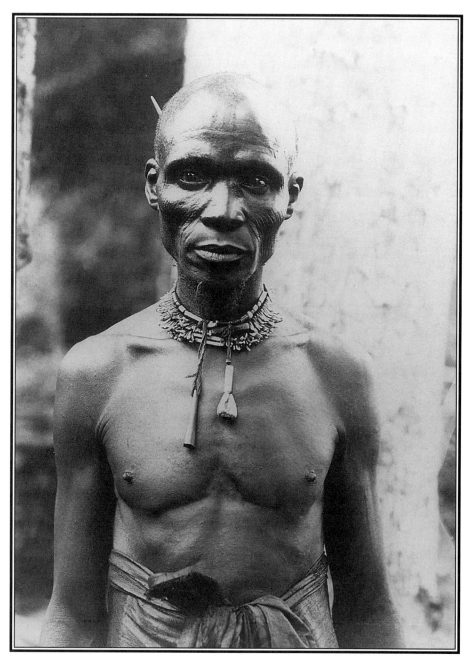

Kwango River Area Chief, c. 1885 *In 1885 George Grenfell photographed this Kwango River area chief. The Kwango is one of the many Congo tributaries. Today Bandundu, about 185 miles northeast of Kinshasa, is the chief city in the region. It is a river port at the junction of the Kwango and Kwilu rivers. The locality produces for export palm oil and fibrous plants used in ropemaking.*

The Self~Made Man

Henry Morton Stanley shook his head in dismay. He could not believe how blind the English government was being to the perfect opportunity to seize control of a huge chunk of Africa. Stanley had recently returned to England from his trek of more than two years across the interior of that continent. On August 12, 1877, when he and what was left of his African party traveled on the steamship *Kabinda* out into the Atlantic Ocean, he had become the first white person to successfully trace the route of the Congo River to its mouth along the western coast of Africa.

Stanley recognized the opportunities that existed in Central Africa for Europeans both to expand their areas of influence and to benefit from a huge supply of natural resources and cheap labor. Like most white people of his day, he did not consider the rights of the people living in the region. He thought of whites as a morally and intellectually superior race who should control the world.

He also felt great loyalty to his homeland, England, in spite of the fact that he was passing himself off as an American. He wanted to give his people the opportunity to make use of his discoveries. However, if they persisted in refusing to seize the moment, he would look elsewhere for a patron. Life had taught Henry Stanley one lesson: he needed to take care of himself, because no one else would.

The first encounter with this harsh reality came early in Stanley's life. He had been born on January 28, 1841, in the small Welsh town of Denbigh and named John Rowlands. His mother, Betsy Parry, was not married, and no one knows who his father was. In those days, being "illegitimate" carried a strong stigma. Disgraced by her unwed status, Betsy Parry fled Denbigh shortly after John's birth. She left her baby with his two uncles and his maternal grandfather.

When John was five, his grandfather died. His uncles paid a local family to take John in. This arrangement worked for about a year. Then the foster family asked for more pay. The uncles refused. The foster family resolved this impass by turning over six-year-old John to the care of the St. Asaph Union Work-house. He would live there for the next nine years. Already John had been abandoned by his mother, his uncles, and a foster family. The stigma of being illegitimate was now reinforced by the disgrace of growing up in a workhouse.

Life at St. Asaph's was hard. The master of the workhouse was known for being an alcoholic and mistreating his staff. The facility was overcrowded, and physical abuse was common. But while dormitory life may have been difficult, John Rowlands thrived in the schoolroom. He loved geography and did so well in his studies that he was awarded a prize Bible by the local bishop.

One evening when John was 12 years old, his supervisor pointed out a tall woman in the dining hall and asked John if he recognized her. Years later, he recorded the event in his autobiography:

> "No, sir," I replied.
> "What, do you not know your own mother?"
> I started, with a burning face, and directed a shy glance at her, and perceived she was regarding me with a look of cool, critical scrutiny. I had expected to feel a gush of tenderness towards her, but her expression was so chilling that the valves of my heart closed as with a snap.

John's mother stayed at the workhouse for a few weeks and then left. Once again, he felt rejected.

When John was 15, he quit St. Asaph's and lived with various relatives. They hated being associated with their workhouse cousin. By age 17 John was living with an uncle in Liverpool, England, and working as a delivery boy for a butcher. He felt one step away from being turned out. When taking some meat to an American merchant ship, he caught the eye of the captain. The older man asked John to sail with them. The young man quickly accepted.

In February 1859, after a seven-week voyage, the ship landed in New Orleans. John jumped ship and began a new life. He approached a cotton broker and asked if he wanted a boy to work for him. Impressed by John's prize Bible with the inscription from the bishop, the man hired him. Not too long after this, John Rowlands decided that he needed a new name to fit his new life. He finally settled on Henry Stanley, the same name as the cotton broker. Eventually he chose "Morton" as his middle name, and Henry Morton Stanley was born.

Stanley was creative about more than names. He also developed a tendency to exaggerate events, sometimes to the point where they bore no relationship to reality. In his autobiography he claimed to have lived with the Stanleys, describing the touching scene of Mrs. Stanley dying from yellow fever. There are two problems with this account: (1) city directories and census reports show Henry Morton Stanley living in one boarding house after another, and (2) Mrs. Henry Stanley did not die until 1878, many years after Henry Morton Stanley left New Orleans.

The Civil War broke out two years after Henry Morton Stanley arrived in the United States. He quickly joined the Confederate Army and in April 1862 fought with his regiment of Arkansas Volunteers at the Battle of Shiloh. He was captured by Union soldiers and sent to a prisoner-of-war camp outside Chicago. As soon as he discovered that the only way out of the crowded, disease-infested prison was to join the Union Army, he enlisted. Eventually he became a ship's clerk in the Union Navy

Native Chief, Lualaba River Area, c. 1885 *The 1,100-mile Lualaba River is one of the principal sources of the mighty Congo. The Lualaba flows into the Congo at the famous 60-mile Boyoma (Stanley) Falls, where the river's elevation sharply drops through seven dramatic waterfalls. Today a railroad goes around the falls, connecting river ports at Kisangani (formerly Stanleyville), the nation's major inland port after Kinshasa, and Ubundu.*

Perhaps the first white man to view the Lualaba River was the Scottish explorer David Livingstone in 1867. His goal was to locate the source of the Congo River and to disprove the hypothesis that the Congo and Nile both flowed from a single great lake in the heart of Africa. Ten years later Sir Henry Morton Stanley successfully navigated the Lualaba down to the great cataracts—and then the Congo on to the coast. Stanley described this epic journey in Through the Dark Continent *(1878).*

In the 1880s the Reverend George Grenfell (1849–1906), using Stanley's records, continued exploring the many sources of the Congo River. However, his primary work was that of a missionary as he had been sent to Africa by the British Baptist Missionary Society. In addition to his evangelistic zeal, Grenfell greatly contributed to mapping the perplexing course of the Congo and its many tributaries. In 1887 the Royal Geographical Society awarded Grenfell its prestigious Patron's Medal in recognition of his important contribution to geography. This 1885 photograph is one of the earliest of the Lualaba River area native peoples. The chief (left), wearing a leopard skin, and his aide (lower right) are pictured with two of Grenfell's guides.

and was on the *Minnesota* when it bombarded a Confederate fort. This made Stanley one of the few people to experience combat on both sides of the war.

In 1865 Stanley deserted the Union Army and began a career as a reporter. His ability to exaggerate helped him write riveting stories. Knowing that Americans were highly biased against the British, Stanley represented himself as an American and carefully hid his Welsh accent. Two years later, his inflammatory coverage of the Indian Wars captured the attention of James Gordon Bennett Jr., publisher of the *New York Herald*. Bennett sent Stanley to cover a British government expedition against Abyssinia, now known as Ethiopia.

Stanley bribed the chief telegraph clerk at Suez to make sure his reports were sent out first. Just after Stanley's account of British victory was transmitted over the wires, the trans-Mediterranean cable broke. His story would appear days before any competitor's account. Stanley soon received word that he had been named roving foreign correspondent for the *Herald*. His new base would be London.

Stanley took note of the increasing British interest in Africa. Along with many other European nations, Britain was looking for a source of raw materials for its factories. It also wanted to end the slave trade and spread Christianity.

The quintessential British explorer was David Livingstone. He was already famous for his missionary work, his antislavery stand, and the almost 30 years he had spent exploring the continent. But when Stanley arrived in London, no one knew where David Livingstone was. His latest expedition had begun in 1866, and people were beginning to wonder what had happened to him. Stanley's boss saw an opportunity. In 1869 he ordered Stanley to travel to Africa and find Livingstone. Stanley broke the news to his fiancée and began planning the trip.

It took two years for Stanley to travel to the east coast of Africa, organize supplies, and hire porters, armed guards, cooks, a guide, and an interpreter. By that time, no one had heard from Livingstone for five years. Stanley was determined to solve the mystery.

Two Women, Lualaba River Area, c. 1885 *George Grenfell photographed these two women showing their tribal scarification. Creating decorative patterns of scars on the skin is a traditional custom in parts of Africa. It is done to beautify the face and body. It is also a sign of social status.*

He was a driven man, who became known for his brutality toward Africans. "When mud and wet sapped the physical energy of the lazily-inclined," he wrote, "a dog-whip became their backs, restoring them to a sound—sometimes to an extravagant—activity." He also wrote of flogging deserters and putting them in chains.

Eight months later, he found his quarry and made his famous statement, "Dr. Livingstone, I presume?" In the meantime, he kept readers around the world entertained with his dispatches, carried out by messengers. The *New York Herald*'s publisher, James Bennett, was ecstatic over reader response.

It is likely that Stanley exaggerated his experiences, but no other version of the journey exists to use for comparison. The two white men traveling with Stanley died during the expedition, and no one interviewed the African porters who survived. David Livingstone chose to remain in Africa. Stanley's newspaper stories and subsequent book, *How I Found Livingstone,* made him world famous and forever linked his name with the African continent. In spite of his success, Stanley was stung by the pain of rejection once again when he returned to England only to discover that his fiancée had married someone else.

In 1874 Livingstone died, and his body was returned to England. Stanley was one of the pallbearers at the funeral. He soon came up with the idea of completing Livingstone's geographic investigations of Central Africa and gained joint sponsorship from the *New York Herald* and the *Daily Telegraph* of London. Basic questions such as the source of the Nile River and the course of the Congo River remained to be answered. Stanley was determined to lay a new claim to fame as the person who completed the work of the revered David Livingstone.

About 1,200 men applied to be part of the trek, including many experienced travelers. Never comfortable around people who were as skilled as he, Stanley chose three inexperienced men to join his party. Two were fishermen and one was a hotel clerk.

Just before he left on what promised to be a long and arduous journey, the 33-year-old Stanley got engaged to a 17-year-old American heiress named Alice Pike. They set a wedding date, and he wrote to her faithfully.

Stanley and his three companions traveled to Zanzibar, an island off the eastern coast of Africa, and organized the expedition. From the island, they would travel to the continent and begin their trek toward the interior of Africa. At the beginning of their journey, the group numbered 356 people, and they carried more than 16,000 pounds of arms, equipment, and goods to be used in trade. The weapons were used frequently. Whenever Stanley perceived a threat, his answer was to shoot. "We have attacked and destroyed 28 large towns and three or four score villages," he wrote.

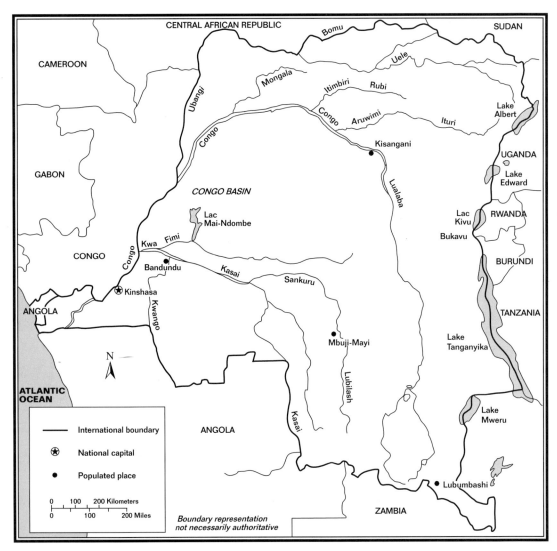

Drainage of the Congo River

African porters carried the supplies. After months of such hard work, many of them mutinied. They stole some of what they carried and disappeared into the rain forest. Stanley was swift and severe in meting out punishment to the remaining men. Drunkards were given 100 lashes and kept in chains for six months. When smallpox broke out, he refused to let sick porters rest and recover or go off into the forest to die. He insisted that they keep at their jobs until they literally dropped dead.

Group of Congolese with Drums, c. 1905 *This photograph was taken by the Congo Press Bureau, which King Leopold personally created in 1904. The aim of the Bureau was to produce and subsidize pro-Leopold stories in the European and American Press.*

The King hired Mary French Sheldon, a London travel writer, whose enthusiastic articles about Leopold's work in the Congo appeared in many British newspapers. "I have witnessed more atrocities in London streets than I have seen in the Congo," she wrote in a 1905 Times *story.*

Stanley's three white companions did not fare well, either. One died of what were called anguish fits. Another became delirious and died. The third drowned in the Congo River. The trip was hard on Stanley as well. Over the course of two and a half years, he lost 60 pounds.

He pushed his rapidly decreasing entourage to follow the Lualaba River, confirming that it indeed was the beginning of

Congolese Man and Child, c. 1905 *This is another photograph taken by King Leopold's Congo Press Bureau. Several British newspapers printed pro-Leopold items from "a most reliable source" or a "well-informed source." Were these newspapers paid to print these stories? We do not know, as the main work of the bureau was done anonymously. We do know that the Congo Press Bureau subsidized an Edinburgh magazine called* New Africa. *Between 1905 and 1907 more than two dozen pamphlets appeared in English praising the Belgian king's Congo programs. Leopold's British publicist, Lieutenant Colonel James Harrison, "a country gentleman of absolutely independent mind, a sportsman and a traveler, and a familiar figure in London Social and Political Circles," wrote that he found "the natives cheerful and satisfied." Despite these efforts at propaganda, the outpouring of criticism of the king's Congo policies continued.*

the Congo River. They noted the many tributaries that gave the Congo the local name of *Nzadi,* meaning "the river that swallows all rivers." The group survived snake and hippo attacks, disease, and worms that burrowed into the porters' feet. They portaged around impassable rapids and waterfalls and crossed the steep and rugged Crystal Mountains. Several times they ran dangerously short of drinking water. Only 116 of the original 356 people lived to see the journey's end. Some of those died a short time later.

Despite the hardships—and the news that, once again, his fiancée had married someone else—Stanley was elated at his final discovery. If a land route could be built around the falls near the mouth of the Congo, the river and its many tributaries would become the major route to the interior of Africa. Fame and money awaited. Yet, Britain failed to avail itself of the opportunity to obtain the riches in the Congo basin, so Henry Stanley turned to someone else. This person had been quietly and cleverly courting Stanley's trust since the explorer began making his way home from Africa. On June 10, 1878, Stanley took a steamship across the English Channel to his first meeting with Leopold II, king of the Belgians.

In the preface to the 1899 edition of his book, *Through the Dark Continent,* Stanley described King Leopold as a man "whose wonderful character and extraordinary ability were then unknown to the world." Like many other people dependent on the good will of a sponsor, Henry Stanley portrayed Leopold in a way that did not match the real man. For just as Stanley was a master at exaggerating events to better serve his purposes, Leopold II had no peer in his ability to cloak greed and evil in the guise of nobility and humanitarian generosity.

Loango Women, c. 1926 *The kingdom of Loango, now southwestern Congo, was one of the oldest and largest in the region. The kingdom reached its fullest power in the late seventeenth century, largely as a result of slave trade. Portuguese slave dealers traveled far inland and returned with cargoes of slaves usually procured for them by the Teke people. The Loango coastal chiefs, who controlled the area of what is now the river port cities of Brazzaville and Kinshasa, levied fees on the Portuguese. The suppression of the slave trade in the nineteenth century hastened the collapse of the Loango kingdom. These Loango women have stone darts in their lower lips.*

2

Dreams of Glory

As he neared his first meeting with Leopold II, Henry Stanley had no idea of the king's expectations of him. Leopold was a frustrated man. He was king of a small, powerless European nation. Even within his own nation, Leopold had limited authority. European monarchies did not hold the absolute power they once had.

The king was determined to become a person of influence and power, and he knew that he possessed two gifts that would help him accomplish his dreams: inherited wealth and an ability to manipulate people. His ability to use people developed at an early age. In part it grew from the necessity of finding his way in a court where the king and queen didn't like him. Born in Brussels on April 9, 1835, Leopold was a disappointment to his parents. His mother constantly pointed out his faults, and his father, Leopold I, communicated to him through secretaries. To see his father, the prince had to apply for a formal audience.

Knowing he could not look to his parents for support, Leopold recognized that many people wanted his favor because he would be the next king. Through these officials, he learned how government worked and saw documents and the latest maps from around the world. His father recognized his skills. "Leopold is subtle and sly," the king told a minister. "He never takes a chance. The other day . . . I watched a fox which wanted to cross a stream unobserved: first of all he dipped a paw carefully to see how deep it was, and then, with a thousand precautions, very slowly made his way across. That's Leopold's way!"

As was expected, Leopold's marriage formed a political alliance. His wife was Archduchess Marie-Henriette, a member of the Hapsburg family, rulers of the Austro-Hungarian Empire. The couple hated each other on sight. This unhappy situation gave Leopold one more reason to lose himself in his studies. When he was 27, he spent a month in Seville studying records of the Spanish conquest of the Americas. He walked away with one lesson: colonialism could bring huge profits to the conquering country.

Leopold noted that neighboring Holland had not let its small size keep it from acquiring colonies. Coffee, sugar, indigo, and tobacco raised in Java provided profits that had built railroads and canals in Holland. Leopold was frustrated that no one in Belgium shared his passion for seizing a colony. The young prince was also ambitious for personal power. Every day he saw signs of his father, the king, losing power. What would there be for Leopold to inherit? He described Belgium as a "small country with small people."

Leopold inherited his small country in 1865 when his father died. The son was 30 years old at the time and restless. His unhappy marriage added to his frustrations. In 1869 his only son died from pneumonia. Although Queen Marie-Henriette had given birth to three other children, they were all girls, and Leopold believed that thrones and royal power should go only to men.

Lacking a colony and a son, King Leopold poured his energies into building projects in Belgium. He created monuments, vast parks, and beautiful palaces. But these accomplishments did not satisfy his need for power. He therefore continued looking for a colony. Africa was the one continent with large areas of unclaimed land, so Leopold focused his colonial plans there. However, it was necessary to disguise those colonial aspirations. The larger European powers would quickly squelch any open grabs for territory from little Belgium. Moreover, the Belgian people had no interest in becoming a colonial power. Consequently, Leopold disguised his intentions in Africa by presenting himself as a philanthropist with an interest in advancing geographic knowledge and ending the slave trade.

His first step was to plan a conference of explorers and geographers for the fall of 1876. Then he visited his cousin Queen Victoria and met with British leaders in missions and geography. He quickly learned what Henry Stanley would later find out: Britain had no interest in the Congo basin. When he recognized that fact, the Congo became King Leopold's target.

Returning to Belgium, the 41-year-old king hosted his geographic conference. He housed his guests in the Royal Palace and greeted them in the throne room, which was lighted by 7,000 candles. He announced his philanthropic intentions, proclaiming that piercing "the darkness which hangs over entire peoples, is, I dare say, a crusade worthy of this century of progress." He also underscored Belgium's neutrality, its small size, and its contentment with this situation. He concluded by saying "I have no other ambition than to serve her well."

The guests—as well as dignitaries throughout the world—were completely taken in. At the close of the meeting, they formed the International African Association (IAA), with King Leopold as its head. Wealthy families contributed money to advance the cause. Praise of Leopold's humanitarian work rang in his ears.

A short while later, the king learned of Henry Stanley's successful expedition and his discoveries about the Congo River basin. Stanley would need a patron. Leopold took steps to be perfectly positioned to take that role. First he sent Stanley a congratulatory telegram. Then he sent personal emissaries to speak with Stanley as he made his way back to England. They offered him a job with the IAA, which Stanley turned down. Once Stanley arrived in England, King Leopold had his minister in London lunch with the explorer. He had people drop hints

Leopold II (1835–1909), king of the Belgians, established the Congo Free State, which he ruled with an iron hand.

that the king might offer the job with the IAA to someone else. Five months later Stanley was ready to talk with the king.

In the meantime, King Leopold had read everything he could find about Stanley's expedition and had drawn some conclusions. The Congo and its tributaries would provide transportation routes once the problem of the rapids was solved. The people living in the region were easily controlled with rifles—good news to the king, because he could not afford a war.

The first meeting between Stanley and King Leopold went well. Leopold spoke fluent English and had a better knowledge of the scope of Stanley's accomplishments than many of the British officials with whom the explorer had spoken. Within a year the two men reached an agreement. Stanley signed a five-year contract to work for the king in the Congo. Leopold would provide all the support personnel. It was essential that no one know of the commercial aspects of the work. Those hired for the mission signed agreements that forbid them from saying anything about what they were doing. When asked for details, Stanley simply said they were involved in "scientific exploration."

Once Stanley set off for the Congo, Leopold concentrated his efforts on reinforcing his image as a humanitarian. He bought out the other shareholders in the IAA, bringing an end to its official existence, but continued to refer to it as if it were still active. He then named his African operations the International Association of the Congo (IAC). Many people assumed that the IAC and the IAA were one and the same. King Leopold let them remain misinformed.

He used others in his disinformation campaign. General Henry Sanford, an American who worked for the king, said that the king wanted to create a chain of stations where travelers could receive scientific information and aid. He stressed the king's desire to end slave traffic. People in Britain were told that the king's aim was to advance progress in this uncivilized region. The image of "free Negro republics" was passed on to Americans, while Europeans were told of "free cities." The king, of course, had no intention of giving any political power to the Africans whose territory he was claiming. But it served his purpose to create that illusion for the rest of the world.

While the king bolstered his image as the great humanitarian, Stanley carved out a road through the Crystal Mountains and around the 220 miles of rapids near the mouth of the Congo. It took two years. Then African porters carried 50 tons of supplies and equipment up the trail. Two reassembled steamships were put into use on the river above the rapids. Stanley subsequently traveled up the river to establish a series of stations that would reinforce Leopold's claim to the territory.

Stanley drove his men mercilessly and pushed the Africans even harder. The best punishment for Africans, he maintained, was putting them in irons because it filled them with both shame and discomfort. Under increasing pressure from the king, Stanley put more pressure on his workers. He reinforced his orders with the threat of his private army—equipped with 1,000 quick-firing rifles, a dozen small cannons, and four machine guns.

By the time Stanley's five-year contract had expired, he had established stations up and down the Congo River. He claimed to have signed contracts with more than 450 Congo basin chiefs. These treaties gave King Leopold a trade monopoly and rights to all land and resources. They gained the Africans next to nothing. No one bothered to make sure the chiefs understood the significance of the documents on which they were marking their Xs. Almost every treaty promised that the chief would assist the association "by labour or otherwise." In effect, the chiefs were giving their people as slaves.

Leopold knew these treaties would be meaningless if his control of the territory was not recognized by world powers. First he used General Sanford to lobby important members of the U.S. government. Sanford assured officials that the area would be open to trade from anyone. His work was successful, and in April 1884 the United States became the first government to recognize King Leopold II's claim to the Congo.

The second country to recognize Leopold's claim was France. That nation worried that when King Leopold inevitably ran out of money to run the colony, Britain might take over. Leopold offered the French a right of first refusal, and they quickly accepted. With slightly more effort, King Leopold convinced Chancellor Bismark of Germany to recognize his claim, once again with guarantees of free trade.

Meanwhile Bismark offered to host a conference in Berlin where the European powers could discuss some of their conflicting claims over parts of Africa. Although Leopold himself did not attend the meeting, which started on November 15, 1884, he saw it as an opportunity to tighten his hold on the Congo. Before the representatives met, he suggested to the British that if he didn't get all the land he wanted in the Congo basin, he would pull out of Africa entirely and would sell the area to the French under the terms of the agreement he had made with them. That was the last thing Britain wanted, so its representatives supported Leopold's claims at the conference, which lasted into February 1885. When it ended, Leopold's claims to the Congo were formally recognized. The 50-year-old monarch had his long desired colony. He was the uncontested proprietor of an area more than 76 times the size of Belgium. On May 29, 1885, the king named his privately controlled country the Congo Free State. He was ready to complete the infrastructure needed to exploit its riches.

Within two years, surveyors were at the mouth of the Congo, beginning to chart the route for a railroad designed to follow the existing road around the rapids. Meanwhile the king was looking for financing. He had inherited vast wealth, but even that was insufficient to fund the infrastructure that was needed.

For a while Leopold made do with bank loans and small investors, but he needed a large loan from Belgium—something he would not easily gain.

At the time, anger among Europeans against the slave trade in central and eastern Africa was reaching a fever pitch. Conveniently, the traders were largely Muslim and either Arab or African, which fed European biases against people who had different cultures or religious beliefs. Leopold joined in this outcry, donated money to Christian missionaries in the Congo Free State, and was elected honorary president of the Aborigines Protection Society, a British human rights organization.

In November 1889 Brussels became the site of an Anti-Slavery Conference of the major European powers. Leopold saw his opportunity. He suggested that armed troops could fight the slave traders. They would, of course, need roads, railways, steamboats, and fortified stations where they could stay. He offered the conferees use of the Congo and in exchange simply asked that he be allowed to levy import duties to finance the attacks. The European powers agreed, ending any earlier guarantees he had made of free trade in the Congo.

Belgian cabinet members were impressed with their king's philanthropic work—and they began to understand that true wealth lay in the Congo. When the king asked Parliament for a loan that would equal about $125 million today, they gave it to him interest free. In exchange, the king promised to deed the Congo to Belgium in his will. When the king made his will public, he dated it before Parliament's action so that the grant appeared to be a generous gesture with no connection to the sizeable loan he had just received.

As King Leopold entered the 1890s, he was lauded internationally as one of the world's great humanitarians. He had his colony. He had access to great wealth. But all that was about to be put at risk. An African American was ready to shock the world with the real story of the Congo Free State and King Leopold.

Congo River Steamer, 1910 *Joseph Conrad (1857–1924), the Polish-born English writer, described his Congo adventures in* Heart of Darkness, *one of his most famous stories. At age 32, in 1889, Conrad obtained work on a Congo River steamer believing at first that King Leopold's mission in Africa was a noble and civilizing one. The Congo Free State was four years old, but it had already become notorious as a sphere of imperialistic exploitation. Conrad's 1902 short story conjured up an atmosphere of horror, treachery, greed, and exploitation. "Before the Congo," wrote Conrad, "I was a mere animal."*

> *Going up that river was like traveling back to the earliest beginnings of the world, when vegetation rioted on the earth and the big trees were kings. An empty stream, a great silence, an impenetrable forest. The air was warm, thick, heavy, sluggish. There was no joy in the brilliance of sunshine. The long stretches of the waterway ran on, deserted, into the gloom of the overshadowed distances. On silvery sandbanks, hippos and alligators sunned themselves side by side. The broadening water flowed through a mob of wooded islands. You lost your way on the river as you would in a desert and butted all day long against shoals trying to find the channel till you thought yourself bewitched and cut off forever from everything you had known.*

3

CRIMES AGAINST HUMANITY

George Washington Williams was a determined and gifted African American whose passion for the Congo exceeded even Leopold's. The two men first met in the fall of 1889 when Williams traveled to Europe as a correspondent. One of his first assignments was to interview King Leopold.

The king soon had Williams under his spell. In his account of their meeting, the American reported that Leopold "proved himself a good listener as well as a pleasant and entertaining conversationalist." The king insisted that he had only two motives for developing the Congo: the selfish motive of trade and commerce, and the noble motive of carrying Christian civilization to Africa.

Leopold was particularly careful to emphasize Christianity because he knew that George Washington Williams had been a successful minister and noted chronicler of black history in America before he had pursued a career in journalism. When Williams pressed the king about what he personally hoped to gain from his investment of time and money, the reply was emphatic, "What I do there is done as a Christian duty to the poor African; and I do not wish to have one franc back of all the money I have expended."

These were the same carefully constructed lies Leopold had been telling for years. But this time the king misjudged the character of his listener. The man sitting across from him had his own dreams for Africa and would soon make plans to visit the Congo to see if the king's words were true.

Who was this man who would shake Leopold's world? George Washington Williams was born in Bedford Springs, Pennsylvania, on October 16, 1849. His parents were poor, but they were determined to make a better future for their children. Their search for new employment opportunities took the family to New Castle, a small town north of Pittsburgh. Though Williams had little formal education as a child, he was exposed to Christianity at an early age when his father became the part-time minister of a black church. That influence did not keep the young man from becoming a teenager who was restless, wildly undisciplined, and endlessly drawn to excitement.

In August 1864, 14-year-old George Williams enlisted in the Union Army. He lied about his age and used an assumed name. He fought in several battles before the end of the Civil War and was wounded, though not seriously. After the war, Williams left the army and traveled to Mexico to fight against the forces of Emperor Maximilian. By the end of 1867, he had returned from Mexico, reenlisted in the U.S. Army, and was stationed at Fort Riley, Kansas. A gunshot wound to his left lung left him unfit for further military duty.

Williams was drawn back to his religious roots. In 1869, after a period of spiritual self-examination, he applied for admission to the newly established Howard University. His "application" was a long autobiographical letter addressed directly to General Oliver Otis Howard, the school's founding president. The letter is the earliest piece of William's writing that has survived and reveals important things about his personality and character. It is breathtakingly bold, bursting with energy and confidence, even a bit reckless at times. Its most remarkable trait is the raw eloquence of its style, which comes through clearly in spite of terrible handwriting, poor grammar, and many spelling errors.

"Sir Mr. Howard," it begins, "i have the Honour to inform and Enterduce my Self witch you an to let you now my Hartes

Desire. an in a Brief Discorel. I will make my Self none to you as one wanting to Be useful to my fellowmen."

Williams was accepted. Less than 20 years old, he was already a master at using powerful patrons in efforts to reach his goals. He convinced General Howard to support his application for a disability pension from the government based on a wound he had received while in combat near Fort Arbuckle, Indian Territory. Williams also had developed a disturbing tendency to exaggerate his accomplishments. He never was granted a pension because the official record stated that he had not been wounded in combat.

Perhaps it is not surprising that Williams did not remain at Howard very long. In the fall of 1870 he applied for admission to the Newton Theological Institution, near Boston. The school had an outstanding faculty and was known for its two-level course structure, which allowed students with little or no college experience to begin studying to be ministers. Williams entered as a general student and spent two years filling the gaps in his rudimentary education. He then completed three years of graduate studies in only two years. Somehow, he found time to fall in love. Shortly before graduation in June 1874, he married Sarah A. Sterrett.

Immediately after graduation Williams became pastor of the Twelfth Baptist Church, the most important black congregation in Boston. Soon his interests changed. Williams had seen and heard a great deal about the suffering of blacks in America. He could not be satisfied with a comfortable position in an established church when other blacks were being subjected to bondage and terror.

In the fall of 1875 he left Boston to found a national black newspaper in Washington, D.C. Williams received enthusiastic support from people such as Frederick Douglass. The first issue of *The Commoner* appeared in September 1875, but the economic and political climate of the country was unfavorable to a black newspaper. It closed before the year ended.

Within a few months Williams had accepted a job as the pastor of the Union Baptist Church of Cincinnati. His life became a tangle of overlapping careers and competing interests. He began as a pastor and civic leader but also worked as a newspaper correspondent and publisher. Eventually he studied law so that he could pursue a career as a politician. In October 1879, at the age of 30, Williams became the first black ever elected to the Ohio General Assembly. During his single term (1880–81) he was an effective legislator, but he had a strange gift for stumbling into controversy. By the early 1880s he had also developed a reputation for financial mismanagement. At the same time, his reputation as a gifted orator grew.

For about two years after he left the Ohio legislature, Williams traveled widely, working on a monumental history of blacks in America. He hoped to use his academic gifts to gain his people a new respect and understanding in a society that seemed determined to ignore both their suffering and their contributions to the nation. The *History of the Negro Race in America from 1619 to 1880* is a carefully researched documentary history that set the standard for future work on the subject and gained immediate recognition even among white scholars. But that fame did not bring relief to Williams's already shaky finances. Because of his financial problems, Williams pursued his work as a lecturer more vigorously and moved to Massachusetts, where he worked as a lawyer. Then, in 1884, Williams learned of King Leopold's plans for the Congo. He wrote to one of Leopold's aides, suggesting that work in Africa might solve the obstacles to progress that blacks faced in America.

By 1886 years of instability and long periods spent away from home had destroyed Williams's marriage and weakened his health. That July he sought a divorce. Although he didn't get the divorce, he and his wife lived apart.

Williams was not ready to give up on life. He was fascinated by the possibilities of the Congo and added it to his lecture topics. In 1889 he traveled to Europe on an assignment to write a series of articles. It was then that he had his first meeting with King Leopold. He also made arrangements with a Belgian company to take 40 skilled artisans to the Congo. When black students in America asked him questions about the colony that he couldn't answer, Williams decided to visit the Congo himself.

George Washington Williams (1849–1891) was a prominent African-American historian, journalist, and clergyman. Originally an admirer of Leopold's Congo policies, Williams was shocked at the problems he saw when he visited the Congo in 1890.

Of course, to do that, he needed money. Williams asked American railroad baron Collis P. Huntington for support. At first Huntington refused, but, probably because of the investment he had already made in the railroad to be built around the rapids on the lower Congo, he eventually made a small donation.

The following December Williams met with President Benjamin Harrison to tell him of his plans to go to Africa. He later used the visit to imply that he was carrying out an important mission for America's leader.

Worried about Williams's activities, Leopold first warned the young man of dangers he might meet and then suggested that a five-year delay would lead to all his expenses being met by the king. Williams replied that he was leaving in a few days.

From January 1890 to the beginning of the next year, Williams sailed around the entire African continent and spent six months in the Congo. The slow journey by both foot and steamer up the Congo River gave plenty of time for him to use his powers of observation. His notebooks grew thick with entries on the conditions he found among the people of the Congo and its tributaries. By the time he reached Stanley Falls, a 1,200 mile journey, he could contain his rage no longer. On July 18, 1891, Williams wrote "An Open Letter to His Serene Majesty Leopold II, King of the Belgians and Sovereign of the Independent State of Congo." His long letter began carefully and respectfully, but the mood soon changed. By the sixth paragraph he accused Leopold of gaining control over the Congo through manipulation and deception and then gave specific examples.

Having shown how easily Leopold and his supporters tricked the Africans, Williams devoted the rest of the Open Letter to the deceit perpetrated against people in Europe and America. He pointed out that promised schools, hospitals, housing, and training had not materialized. "Your Majesty's Government has never spent one franc for educational purposes, nor instituted any practical system of industrialism," he charged.

Next Williams described the restrictions non-Belgians faced in what was supposed to be free trade. Africans who tried to establish trade contacts independent of Belgian control faced violent harassment. Goods were seized, villages were burned, and many enterprising black traders were simply killed.

Williams's main concern remained the abuse of Africans who called the Congo home. Whenever he wrote of those horrors, his writing changed from the careful reasoning of a lawyer to the outraged pronouncement of a biblical prophet calling down the wrath of God. With one shocking example after another, George Washington Williams brought the dark secrets of the Congo Free State into the open. The issue of slavery was woven into many of those stories, and near the end of the letter, he addressed that issue directly: "Your Majesty's Government is engaged in the slave-trade, wholesale and retail. It buys and sells and steals slaves. . . . The labour force at the stations of your Majesty's Government in the Upper River is composed of slaves of all ages and both sexes."

Though he singled out many individuals for blame throughout his letter, in the end Williams held one man personally responsible for the horrors he had uncovered. "All the crimes perpetuated in the Congo have been done in *your* name, and *you* must answer at the bar of Public Sentiment for the misgovernment of a people." Williams closed with an appeal for European governments to end Leopold's unlimited control of the Congo.

Adam Hochshild, author of a recent study of the Congo Free State, calls Williams's Open Letter "the first comprehensive, systematic indictment of Leopold's colonial regime written by anyone." What George Washington Williams had written was powerful and shocking in part because it shifted the discussion about the African continent, making the basic human rights of Africans the primary issue. It forced Europeans and Americans to begin acknowledging how much corruption and greed were hidden in their proud designs to "civilize, Christianize, and uplift" the "backward" peoples of the world.

Williams arranged to have his letter printed in Europe and distributed widely. He also wrote individually to government and business leaders. In his letter to the U.S. secretary of state, he charged Leopold's state with "crimes against humanity."

After Williams completed his African journey on January 21, 1891, he should have been honing his skills as writer and orator to pursue his attack on the king. But Williams was seriously ill with tuberculosis. He took a ship from Egypt to Britain in hopes of recovering. During the voyage he met Alice Fryer, to whom he became engaged.

Meanwhile Leopold was holding urgent meetings to decide how to counter Williams's attacks. He used Williams's financial problems and other personal weaknesses to discredit him. Fortunately for Leopold, the health of his enemy grew steadily worse. In July George Washington Williams traveled to Blackpool with Alice Fryer and her mother in hopes that the sea air would end his illness. On August 2 the end came. Williams was buried in an unmarked grave, identified only by plot number in the cemetery's records.

Williams's enemies rejoiced in his death, but the hypnotic spell Leopold had cast over Europe and America was broken. The slumbering moral consciences of missionaries, diplomats, and business people began to awaken. Williams died too soon to make all of his findings known and to defend himself, but the echoes of his demands for justice remained. In many quarters, an uncomfortable suspicion began to grow that something terrible was going on in the Congo. Soon an even more uncomfortable thought began to occur to a few individuals: perhaps there was something they needed to do about it. It would take a decade before that discomfort would become an unbearable ache and the quiet doubts would become loud cries for change.

Musician, c. 1908 *What is termed traditional African music is probably very different from the African music of former times. African music has not been rigidly linked to specific ethnic groups. Rather, each musician tried to demonstrate individuality and creativity. Émil Torday photographed this Kasai River basin area musician.*

4

The Kingdom of the Kongo

Whe hen Henry Stanley first traveled down the Congo River, he kept a detailed journal from which he later wrote his two-volume book, *Through the Dark Continent.* But his notes give very little information about the culture of the people whose land he passed. He probably didn't consider these Africans to have a culture. Without realizing it, Stanley was encountering the remnants of a once powerful kingdom that had rivaled its European peers in social and political structure as well as in the arts. This kingdom of the Kongo gave its name to both the river and the region. The Kongo people, or Bakongo, spoke a version of Bantu and had migrated to central and western Africa more than a thousand years ago. They formed their kingdom at least 100 years before Portuguese explorers first landed on their western shores in 1482.

At the height of its power, the kingdom of the Kongo directly controlled an area of about 90,000 square miles, covering land that today is in several West African nations, including the Democratic Republic of the Congo and Angola. From the mouth of the Congo River, that control extended north about 100 miles to the mouth of the Kwilu River. It also reached south about 200 miles to the mouth of the Dande

***Grainaries Surrounding Bakongo Village, Between the Loange and Kasai Rivers, Central Congo, c.
1908.*** *Émil Torday, the Belgian explorer, perhaps was the first white man to travel extensively through
the Kasai River basin area in the central Congo, 1907–09. During his three expeditions to the Congo
between 1899 and 1909, Torday compiled a comprehensive grammar of the Bantu languages. He
donated his collection of Congo artifacts to the British Museum. It is an important primary source for
studying the ethnology of the central Congo peoples.*

*Torday wrote that Bakongo villages were practically independent, with little contact occurring
among them. He traveled unarmed, with one companion and about 20 native carriers. "This could not
be avoided," wrote Torday, "because the currency [of the area] was iron bars weighing 2 lbs. each. . . .
I had to carry 100 pounds' worth [and] matches and salt." At first, the natives thought that Torday was
a "ghost"—and demanded he leave by "putting new feathers on their arrows and making new bow-
strings." However, Torday gradually made friends and was allowed to stay for four days.*

*Torday observed that the Bakongo were "extremely reticent and it was impossible to obtain any
information from them as to their past history or present institutions." He noted, though, that each village was fortified by strong wooden stakes. The people were accomplished woodcarvers, and they also
embroidered palmcloth.*

River, near today's city of Luanda, Angola. The kingdom reached inland more than 300 miles, giving it access to Malebo Pool (which one day would became known as Stanley Pool). Its eastern boundary included the Kwango River. Because of trade and other interaction, the economic and political power of the kingdom extended into the surrounding area, giving it a total sphere of influence covering roughly 200,000 square miles.

The artistic achievement of these people was astounding. They mined copper from which they crafted beautiful jewelry, small statues, and fetishes. They also mined iron ore, smelted it, and then shaped it into weapons, tools, ornaments, and musical instruments. Tradition held that the man who founded the kingdom of the Kongo was a blacksmith. Because of this, the nobility did ironwork.

Their weavers excelled. Using leaves from the raffia palm tree, along with other vegetable fibers, they created a variety of materials that the Portuguese at first mistook for velvet, damask, brocade, satin, and taffeta. They even made cloth by beating the bark of trees. Skilled artisans used vines and wicker to create beautiful baskets, nets, and furniture. They carved wood and ivory and combined the two materials in striking pieces of inlaid furniture. Some of the Kongo people specialized in making pottery.

Their kingdom was led by a man called the *maniKongo*. He carried a zebra-tail whip as a sign of authority. The maniKongo ruled over about a half-dozen provinces and appointed governors to oversee them. The Kongo government was made up of highly specialized positions. For example one person served as *mani vangu vangu,* meaning "first judge, in cases of adultery." Like many rulers, the maniKongo collected taxes from his people and controlled the currency supply. He also strengthened his authority and power by marrying women from influential families.

The maniKongo lived in Mbanza Kongo. *Mbanza* means "court." This large town was located on top of a hill with a commanding view of the area. It took about 10 days to walk

The Chief, Bakongo Village, c. 1908 *At one point, Torday wrote, the chief became hostile "when our stock of iron was nearly finished." He told Torday "that the Great Chief had decided to kill us." "I replied [that] I would slay all of his people with my elephant. Of course, the man expressed some doubt as to the existence of an elephant. Fortunately, among the many objects which we carried about with us was a clockwork elephant, which was capable of waving its trunk and humming while walking along. . . . I wound up the elephant and made it walk on some boxes." To further illustrate his power, Torday threatened "to set fire to the rivers"—he illustrated how he would do this by igniting some whiskey. Convinced, the chief had his men carry Torday's loads to the next village.*

from the coast to Mbanza Kongo. The maniKongo was responsible for settling disputes and dispensing justice. No one could approach him without first getting on their hands and knees. Anyone who watched him eat or drink was executed. To prevent this from happening, an attendant struck two iron poles together to warn people that their ruler was about to eat. Everyone in sight immediately dropped to the ground and lay face down.

The Kongo people had developed systems for measuring distances and time. Travel was described in terms of marching days. They used a lunar calendar and had four-day weeks. The first day of each week was a holiday. Although they didn't write and didn't have the wheel, they excelled as farmers and grew yams, bananas, and other fruit and vegetables. They raised pigs, goats, and cattle, and fished from the Congo River. The people also used palm trees for making oil, wine, vinegar, and bread.

As in much of Africa, a type of slavery existed. Slaves usually were people who had been captured during a war, had committed some criminal act, or were given by their families as part of a dowry payment.

Much of our understanding about Kongo culture comes from Nzinga Mbemba, who is known to history as Affonso I. When the Portuguese first made their way to Mbanza Kongo in 1491, he was a provincial governor. He converted to Christianity, took on the name Affonso, and studied with the priests at the capital for 10 years. He became maniKongo in 1506 and ruled for almost 40 years. Through his studies, he had learned to speak fluent Portuguese, and he dictated a series of letters to Portuguese kings. Dozens of those letters still exist, and they provide an amazing source of information about both the culture of the Kongo people and the changes that the arrival of the Portuguese made in their way of life.

Some of those changes Affonso welcomed, even encouraged. He wanted to modernize his kingdom with the best of what the Portuguese brought. He supported the Roman Catholic Church and appreciated the value of European medicine. He wanted his people to incorporate the woodworking and masonry techniques used by the Portuguese, and he saw the written word as a valuable commodity. Of course, European weaponry was eagerly used to put down any unrest within his far-flung territory.

But Affonso used care in what he chose to accept. He turned down suggestions that he adopt the Portuguese legal code, and he was wary of foreign explorers. He figured that if they discovered the gold and silver deposits in his kingdom, these foreigners would take over his kingdom rather than treating him as a partner. And one change introduced by the Portuguese greatly disturbed the king: their form of slavery. Six years before Affonso took power, a Portuguese expedition had been blown off course and landed in what is now Brazil. Portugal realized great profits could be made in this new land, and within a few decades, a huge demand existed for slaves to run Brazil's mines and coffee plantations. Slaves were also used on Caribbean sugar plantations.

The existence of slavery within the kingdom of the Kongo predisposed chiefs to be willing to sell to the slave traders who descended on Western Africa. So much money was available through slave trade that even some of the priests abandoned their calling and began selling their servants and converts into slavery. By the 1530s more than 5,000 slaves a year were being shipped across the Atlantic from a port at the mouth of the Congo River. Some of these came from the kingdom of the Kongo itself. Others were brought by African slave dealers who traveled more than 700 miles inland to buy slaves from local chiefs. They locked the slaves' necks into wooden yokes and force-marched them to the coast. Many died on the way, and their bodies were left beside the trails.

Affonso faced two problems. First, the population of his kingdom was dropping, and his authority was being undermined as village and provincial chiefs became wealthy through the slave trade. They no longer depended on Affonso's goodwill for their power. Second, although he did not seem to understand this at first, the Portuguese government preferred to have the slave trade continue so that it could benefit from the riches of South America. The government was less concerned about keeping agreements to provide Affonso with medicine and technology. In 1526 Affonso wrote a letter to the King João III

Bambala Men, Southwest Congo, c. 1906 *The Bambala people live along the Kwilu River, which is a tributary of the Kasai River in the southwestern Congo. Today Kikwit is the largest town in the area. Population was estimated at 182,000 in 1994. The production of palm oil and peanuts has replaced rubber as the economic base of the region. Unfortunately, in recent years the area has experienced several severe outbreaks of the Ebola virus.*

Kongo Ritual Statues, 1915 *The Kongo, or Bakongo, group of Bantu-speaking people who live close to the Atlantic coast make masks, figures, and other carved objects that show an identifiable styliza- tion. The Kongo religion focuses on ancestor and spirit cults. These two statues, which guard a small village, are supposed to bring good luck in hunting.*

of Portugal:

> The excessive freedom given by your factors and offi-
> cials to the men and merchants who are allowed to come
> to this Kingdom . . . is such . . . that many of our vas-
> sals, whom we had in obedience, do not comply. We can
> not reckon how great the damage is, since the above-

mentioned merchants daily seize our subjects, sons of
the land and sons of our noblemen and vassals and relatives. . . . Thieves and men of evil conscience take them
because they wish to possess the things and wares of
this Kingdom. . . They grab them and cause them to be
sold; and so great, Sir, is their corruption and licentious-
ness that our country is being utterly depopulated . . . to
avoid this, we need from your Kingdoms no other than
priests and people to teach in schools, and no other
goods but wine and flour for the holy sacrament; that is
why we beg your Highness to help and assist us in this
matter, commanding the factors that they should send
here neither merchants nor wares, because it is *our will
that in these kingdoms there should not be any trade in
slaves nor market for slaves.*

This letter, like the many that had preceded it, went unan-
swered. Finally, in 1529, King João responded: "You . . . tell me
that you want no slave-trading in your domains, because this
trade is depopulating your country. . . . The Portuguese there,
on the contrary, tell me how vast the Congo is, and how it is so
thickly populated that it seems as if no slave has ever left."
Affonso sent several letters to the pope, asking him to inter-
vene, but the Portuguese intercepted Affonso's messengers as
soon as they stepped off the ship in Lisbon. By 1539 Affonso
despaired of resolving these problems. He learned that 10 of his
nephews, grandsons, and other relatives whom he had sent to
Portugal for a religious education had never arrived. Somewhere during their voyage, the young men had been carried to
Brazil, where they became slaves. What could he do when the
Portuguese were not even willing to guarantee safe passage for
members of the royal family?

Affonso died in 1542 or 1543. Although other maniKongos
ruled over the kingdom after his death, he was the last ruler
with any hope of protecting his people. As time passed,
provincial and village chiefs paid less attention to the capital.

Mat Weaving, c. 1926 *Reeds are being woven into a mat that can be used for sleeping on or for making baskets. In the Congo region, sculpture and weaving are usually male activities, while women excel in embroidery. The band around this weaver's head denotes mourning for a dead relative.*

They fought among themselves for the riches of the slave trade.

In 1568 a further catastrophe fell upon the Kongo people. The Yakas (or Jagas) attacked from the south and east. The Yakas were a warrior nation whose people lived in small, fortified, mobile camps. They killed their own babies so that their march would not be slowed and adopted the children of their conquered enemies to raise as the next generation of warriors. The Yakas practiced cannibalism as much to terrify their enemies as for any other purpose.

The Yaka attack on the kingdom of the Kongo began in the southwest frontier next to the Kwango River. They marched toward the royal capital, pillaging and plundering on the way. Learning of the Yaka advance, the maniKongo, his nobles, and the Portuguese staying in the capital fled toward the Congo River. The Yakas torched the city and killed and ate whoever remained. Then they broke into regiments that attacked the rest of the kingdom.

Kongo survivors lived on an island at the mouth of the Congo. Slave traders came to the island offering food in exchange for slaves. Fathers sold sons, and brothers sold brothers. Finally the maniKongo was able to get a message to the Portuguese king, who sent 600 soldiers to put down the Yakas. Working with what was left of the maniKongo's forces, the Portuguese took two years to drive the Yakas out of the kingdom.

But little remained for the maniKongo to rule. The Yakas remained a threat in the Congo River basin for years. Every village was in open revolt against the maniKongo, and plague and famine further decimated the population. Slave traders and soldiers of fortune had free run through land that had once been the home of a proud kingdom. By the end of the century, Britain, France, and Holland joined in the slave trade. Roughly one of every four slaves taken to the cotton and tobacco plantations of the British southern colonies came from equatorial Africa.

Pot Making, Belgian Congo, 1925 *This pot is being made by the traditional molding method. Clay pots are used for cooking and for carrying and storing food and water.*

In 1665 the Kongo people made one last effort to expel the Portuguese. Their army lost, and the maniKongo was beheaded. Over the next 200 years, internal conflict and continuing slave trade further weakened the kingdom. Although the slave trade to Europe and the Americas was illegal by the time of Stanley's journey, the people who remained were no longer a united kingdom. They could offer little resistance to King Leopold and the carnage he was about to unleash on their land.

Termite Hill, Belgian Congo, 1920 *The British naturalist S.A. Neave wrote that the driver ants were common throughout the Congo region, especially in the plateau areas and near the water. "They are frequently seen," he wrote, "marching in vast armies, several abreast." "Woe betide the man who is so unlucky as to tread amongst them. He is immediately covered with a host of bloodthirsty enemies, who bury their mandibles in his flesh, producing the sensation of innumerable red-hot needles."*

Neave also described the Congo termite who built "varied and remarkable mounds. Some of them are of enormous size and have a marked influence upon the landscape. They are sometimes as much as 20 feet high, and are frequently placed at somewhat regular intervals about 30 or 40 yards apart. . . . It is a striking sight to see a grassy plain apparently studded with innumerable gray objects looking very much like stalagmites."

5

THE CHILDREN OF THE FOREST

In 1887 Henry Stanley entered what to him seemed a forbidding and mysterious world. The Ituri rain forest in the northeast corner of the Congo basin is extremely humid and filled with trees that reach heights of 170 feet. Their branches form a canopy through which the sun rarely breaks. Roots run down the sides of trees and across the forest floor, posing hazards to unwary travelers making their way along the dimly lit paths. Insects provide unremitting background noise. Cicadas on tree trunks give out an irritating buzz. The sound of army ants advancing in columns and cracking the bodies of insect prey carries through the moist air. To the stranger in the forest, cries of wild animals and exotic birds add to the perception of having entered a threatening environment. Joseph Conrad called the forest the "heart of darkness."

But to one group of people, this forest world was home. Moving through the rain forest with ease, they found within its confines all they needed for survival. These people called themselves the Children of the Forest and worshiped the natural environment as a living being. They lived in a symbiotic relationship with Bantu- and Sudanic-speaking tribes who formed established villages around and in the rain forest, raising crops and animals.

Pygmy Men Holding Poison Arrows and Spears, 1934 *A Pygmy, or Bambuti, is defined as a member of any human group where adult males grow to less than 59 inches in average height. The best known Pygmies live in the Ituri area, a dense tropical rain forest located in the northeastern Congo River basin, slightly west of lakes Albert and Edward near the Ugandan border. The rich soil and heavy rains of the forest, a vast canopy of trees that admits scant sunlight, and sustaining plants and animals provide the Pygmies with their basic needs—food, water, firewood, and clothing.*

The Pygmy people are nomadic hunters and food gatherers practicing neither agriculture nor animal husbandry. Pygmy families live in beehive-shaped huts—crossed sticks over which broad mongongo leaves are layered. These temporary shelters are constructed in a few hours. Several together are called a "band" or "camp." The Pygmy moves their "band" every three weeks to take advantage of the edible plants and animals. These nomadic people carry all their belongings with them in reed baskets. Their days are spent hunting and collecting honey, wild fruits, and edible roots. Bow and arrow are the Pygmy weapons, and most men are skilled marksmen, constantly practicing on monkeys and other small animals. The Pygmy way of life has remained relatively unchanged through the centuries.

Europeans called these forest dwellers *Pygmies* because of their short stature. Today they are named the *Bambuti,* to distinguish them from other short-statured people in Africa. The Bambuti are divided into four groups. The Efe and Mbuti are the two largest, but the Sua and Aka also have created their own ways of living in the forest. The best understood group of the four is the Mbuti. Many experts consider the Bambuti to be our closest direct link to the oldest human populations in Africa.

The existence of the Bambuti has been recorded for millenia. They have always captured the imagination of others. The first written record comes from about 2250 B.C. In a letter to one of his commanders, the Egyptian Pharaoh Nefrikare, Pepi II, appeared excited about the prospect of having one of these people returned to his court. After giving strict warnings about guarding the safety of the captured "dancing dwarf of the god from the land of spirits," he said, "My majesty desires to see this dwarf more than the gifts of Sinai and Punt." [Duffy, p. 18]

The Greek poet Homer, more than 1,300 years later, mentioned Pygmies in his *Iliad,* and the Greek historian Herodotus wrote of people who traveled south across the desert to a forest where they were captured by Pygmies. The Greeks gave Pygmies their name. The word comes from a unit of measure taken from the distance between a man's elbow and his knuckles. Obviously, the Pygmies' short stature was exaggerated.

Over the millenia, the existence of Pygmies has often been relegated to legend, so incredible did it seem to others that such short people could survive in the harsh rain forest. In his *History of Animals,* Aristotle (384–322 B.C.) mentioned Pygmies in connection with cranes who fly to the lakes which the Nile River flows from. "There dwell the Pygmies, and this is no fable," he stated, apparently answering skeptics. Abed bin Juma, an Arabian trader from the first century B.C., spoke of meeting members of a mysterious race of dwarfs who had long been thought of as something from fiction. And early European explorers heard stories about legendary Pygmies from non-Pygmy groups who they encountered in Africa. One story said

that the Pygmies could become invisible, making it easier for them to kill elephants.

In Western Europe and America, the existence of Pygmies was not verified until 1867, when Paul du Chaillu, a French-American explorer, released his book, *A Journey to Ashango-Land.* He described encountering Pygmies in the depths of the rain forest north of the Congo and gave a detailed description of their appearance and way of life. As other explorers, including Stanley, began having encounters with Bambuti, they wrote vivid descriptions that varied in their accuracy. The Bambuti's most obvious feature was their height. The Mbuti are the smallest people in the world. Adult men average four feet, eight and a half inches, and women average four feet, six inches.

Although the Bambuti are hunter-gatherers who rarely stay in one place for as long as a month, each of the four groups that make up the Bambuti stay in certain general areas of the forest. For example, the Efe live in the northern and eastern regions of the forest, while the Mbuti live in the central and

Pygmies with Poison Arrows, 1927 *The Pygmy were among the earliest African inhabitants. They are mentioned and pictured in early Egyptian and Greek records. In fact, the ancient Greeks coined the word* pygmaios, *indicating the distance from elbow to knuckles—their way of emphasizing the extreme shortness of these people. Scholars suspect that the Pygmy once had their own language. If so, it has long since been forgotten in the Ituri Forest. Among themselves they speak a dialect of their Bantu neighbors. Since the Pygmy use their own singsong intonation, even the Bantu find them difficult to understand. One anthropologist, who translated hundreds of legends that the Pygmies chanted, concluded that they were so symbol-laden as to be incomprehensible to non-Pygmies. The legends tell of conflict with animals, nature, and spirits. Lowell Thomas Jr., a world traveler, described how he was awakened in a Pygmy camp by a voice that called out loudly, as if making a speech in the darkness. The next morning, he was told that a Pygmy ancestor, taking the voice of an owl, had spoken from the forest. The voice Thomas heard was that of a Pygmy answering it.*

Every male Pygmy becomes an excellent hunter. They move though the forest so silently that some Bantu believe Pygmies can make themselves invisible. For large game, the archers use arrowheads obtained from Bantu blacksmiths. Slayers of elephants enjoy hero status, for they have passed the ultimate test in courage. For monkey hunting, they use serrated wooden tips dipped in a heart-stopping juice. Henry Morton Stanley, exploring the Congo in 1876–77, reported that a superficial arrow wound killed a man within one minute.

southern portions of the forest. Some customs the four groups hold in common. They hunt in groups that vary in size from 10 to 100 individuals, all of whom usually share a paternal line. The rain forest provides their basic necessities: food, fresh water, firewood, and clothing.

Bambuti ritual and myth always feature the forest. They pass their traditions from one generation to the next through song, dance, mime, and stories. One of the Mbuti legends teaches about the importance of singing. Colin M. Turnbull recorded the story of the Bird with the Most Beautiful Song in his book, *The Forest People:*

> This bird was found by a young boy who heard such a Beautiful Song that he had to go and see who was singing. When he found the Bird he brought it back to the camp to feed it. His father was annoyed at having to give food to the Bird, but the son pleaded and the Bird was fed. The next day the Bird sang again; it sang the Most Beautiful Song in the Forest, and again the boy went to it and brought it back to feed it. This time the father was even more angered, but once again he gave in and fed the Bird. The third day (most Pygmy stories repeat themselves at least three times) the same thing happened. But this time the father took the Bird from his son and told his son to go away. When his son had left, the father killed the Bird, the Bird with the Most Beautiful Song in the Forest, and with the Bird he killed the Song, and with the Song he killed him- self and he dropped dead, completely dead, dead for ever.

Although they don't observe birthdays, the Bambuti mark other occasions. Events such as the rite of passage from child- hood to adulthood, marriage, and death feature songs designed to "rejoice the forest." These songs are rhythmically and har- monically complex.

Marriage involves a sister exchange. If a man wants to marry, he must first arrange a marriage between one of the

Pygmy Warriors, 1926 *King Leopold considered the Pygmies to be human freaks. In 1897 a World's Fair was held in Brussels. More than 1 million people came to see Leopold's exhibits celebrating his concept of the Congo. A pair of Pygmies were on display in a specially constructed forest village.*

Perhaps the most appalling case of an indigenous people placed on exhibit took place at New York's Bronx Zoo in September 1906. A Pygmy was displayed in the monkey house sharing space with an orangutan. Newspaper stories suggested that the Pygmy ate human flesh. To further this impression, the zoo keepers left bones scattered on the floor around him. A poem published in The New York Times *declared that the Pygmy had been brought*

> *From his native land of darkness,*
> *To the country of the free,*
> *In the interest of science*
> *And of broad humanity.*

A group of black ministers finally rescued the Pygmy from the zoo. He remained in the United States and committed suicide ten years later.

**Distribution of Principal
Ethnic Groups**

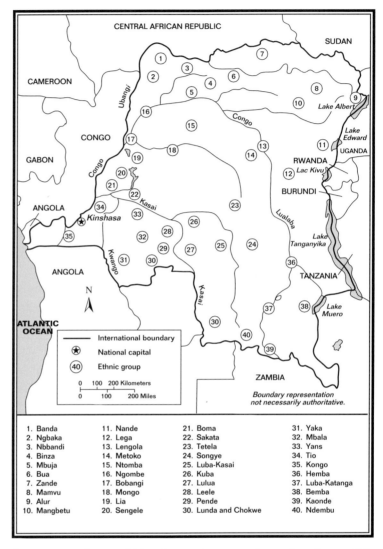

1. Banda	11. Nande	21. Boma	31. Yaka
2. Ngbaka	12. Lega	22. Sakata	32. Mbala
3. Nbbandi	13. Lengola	23. Tetela	33. Yans
4. Binza	14. Metoko	24. Songye	34. Tio
5. Mbuja	15. Ntomba	25. Luba-Kasai	35. Kongo
6. Bua	16. Ngombe	26. Kuba	36. Hemba
7. Zande	17. Bobangi	27. Lulua	37. Luba-Katanga
8. Mamvu	18. Mongo	28. Leele	38. Bemba
9. Alur	19. Lia	29. Pende	39. Kaonde
10. Mangbetu	20. Sengele	30. Lunda and Chokwe	40. Ndembu

female members of his clan and a man from the clan of his prospective bride. Marriage relationships appear to be stable. Men rarely take more than one wife, and the extended family relationships hold the people together.

Privacy is almost unheard of among the Bambuti. They live in huts that the women can construct in about two hours. They first form a beehive-shaped frame of sticks and then cover it with leaves. The huts provide protection from frequent rain but do nothing to insulate sound. Conversations in one hut can easily be heard by people in nearby huts, which are usually arranged in a loose circle around the center of their temporary home site or camp.

The Bambuti possess few things, and what they have is shared with everyone else. They do not have a formal government, nor do they choose chiefs or have a council of elders. They settle problems and disputes through general discussion.

Jobs among the Bambuti are somewhat defined by gender. The men hunt mammals and gather wild honey. The women gather nuts, tubers, and fruits. The men create and repair tools needed for hunting, and the women create and repair baskets and other items needed for gathering.

Some differences exist between the four Bambuti groups. One of the biggest differences is in their mode of hunting. The Efe use bows and arrows for hunting monkeys and forest antelope. When hunting larger game, such as buffalo, giant forest hog, and elephant, they use spears. In contrast, the Mbuti use nets for hunting forest antelope and other small mammals. Mbuti hunting is ritualized. The men go into the forest early in the morning and build a *kungya,* a fire that honors the forest and asks for its blessing on the hunt. While waiting for the women, the men burn small branches and blacken their faces with the burned ends of the sticks. In so doing, they are wearing part of the hunting fire that has been made from the sacred forest. The Mbuti believe such actions will bring them luck in the hunt.

Soon the women arrive, leaving children younger than about age 10 back at the camp where they are looked after by adults old enough to let grown sons hunt for them. The women carry baskets in which they will collect mushrooms and other edibles as well as carry any small animals caught in the hunt. Next the hunters silently choose a spot that contains the type of plants the nocturnal antelope like to hide in during the day. They uncoil their nets, which are made from natural materials and are almost invisible in the dim light of the forest. The nets are suspended from trees or tied to bushes and placed end to end in a half-circle. They are about three and one-half feet high and are designed to catch small antelope and other mammals. The men stay with the nets, waiting for the animals.

At this point, the women take on their traditional role as beaters. They silently move through the forest, getting closer to the animals that are sleeping between the women and the nets. Suddenly the women shout and beat the bushes to startle the animals and drive them toward the nets. The men and older boys wait to spear animals that get tangled in the nets. Once the animals are killed and placed in the baskets, the nets are coiled up, and the group will walk another mile or so and repeat the process.

On the rare occasion when any of the Bambuti kill an elephant, they promptly move their camp to where the elephant lies. It is easier for them to move to the elephant than to move the elephant back to camp.

The Bambuti were self-sufficient until about 400 years ago, when their Bantu- and Sudanic-speaking neighbors probably first arrived in the forest. Each group of Bambuti developed loose trading and cultural ties with a particular farming village. The Bambuti traded meat and honey for bananas, vegetables, and other cultivated crops. Their farming neighbors also introduced the Bambuti to metal knives and spears. Over time, they began to share words and customs with each other. Bambuti women began working in the villagers' fields. The villagers thought of themselves as superior to the Bambuti; in one language the villagers' word for themselves means "master." When ill-treated, however, the Bambuti simply slipped away into the forest and disappeared for months at a time.

After Henry Stanley's first encounter with the Bambuti, European influence began to spread up the Congo River into the Ituri forest. Armed trading stations were established to exploit the people and resources of the northeast Congo basin. New demands fell most heavily on the villagers, because the

Bambuti were not as easy to capture. They could slip away from the Europeans just as they had from the villagers. But some Bambuti were caught, and when they weren't used in forced labor, they were often shipped to European and American cities to be viewed as curiosities. Separated from the forest life and diet they knew, immersed in loud, crowded societies, many of these Bambuti got ill and died. At least one is known to have committed suicide. As long as Europeans searched for wealth along the Ituri forest, the Bambuti way of life was at risk.

Kuba Mashamboy, or Entertainers, c. 1920 *The Kuba made decorated masks and headwear from raffia using shells, beads, and even bells and feathers. These* masham-boy *traditionally dramatize the founding of the royal dynasty. Today the Kuba people keep relatively aloof from modern life. Few have emigrated or engage in European-style occupations.*

6

THE HIDDEN KINGDOM

In 1892 the first African-American missionary to the Congo sat in a precarious position. William Henry Sheppard had taken a party of eight African men and, from a discreet distance, followed an ivory caravan deep into Kuba territory in the interior of the Congo. Bordered on the southwest by the Kasai and Lulua Rivers and on the north by the Sankuru River, the isolation of the Kuba kingdom had protected it for centuries from unwelcome guests.

In every village he had passed, Sheppard had been warned that the king would likely punish him and would definitely punish the people of the villages who allowed him to continue on his journey. Foreigners were not allowed within this area of the Kuba kingdom. But now he had spent a month in a village because he did not know what direction to take next to reach the court of the king of the Kuba, Kot aMbweeky II. What bothered him most was that three more ivory traders had passed through the village as he waited. Even if he followed them, Sheppard knew they would reach the capital, Ifuca, long before he would, because they were familiar with the territory. Once they reached Ifuca, they would likely tell the king of the unauthorized presence of Sheppard's group.

As Sheppard waited, the king's son, Toen-zaide, led a party of 50 armed men down into the village. Immediately, the warriors seized and bound the villagers. Sheppard

**Major States in the
Southern Savannas,
Mid-19th Century**

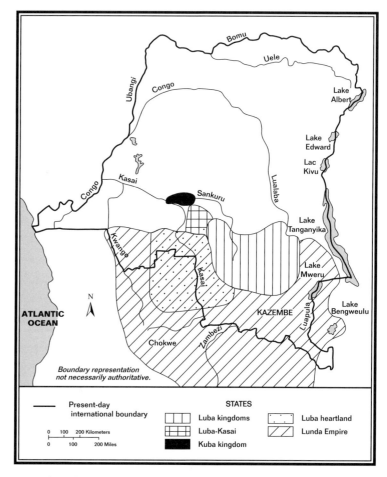

put aside the book he had been reading and asked for the privilege of speaking to Toen-zaide. Told that the prince would speak to him, Sheppard did what he could to show respect to his guest. He spread out a grass mat and a striking piece of woven material for the prince to sit on.

Toen-zaide informed Sheppard that the king had ordered him to take not only the foreigners but also everyone from the village to the court to receive punishment. The punishment would be execution. Sheppard felt it was only right to take full responsibility for his actions and try to protect both the Africans in his party and the villagers with whom he had been staying. Using the Kuba language, the missionary explained how he had received no assistance and had made his own map as he traveled into Kuba territory so that he would be able to find his way out again. Sheppard also said that both his men and the villagers had begged him to turn back.

The prince looked at him in amazement. How could this complete stranger speak their language even though he had never been there before? How could he have penetrated so far into the kingdom without a guide? The prince made a decision. He ordered Sheppard, his party, and the villagers to wait for his return. He would report back to his father about what he had discovered.

As the prince left, Sheppard returned to his book. All he could do was wait. Either he would be welcomed as a guest, or he had brought great danger to many innocent people through his own stubbornness.

The kingdom William Sheppard had so determinedly entered had existed since about 1600. It was a confederation of 18 tribes over which the king ruled. Kuba civilization was well developed, and because it was in the heart of Congo territory, it had escaped the slave trade from both the east and the west. When the Congo Free State was formed in 1885, the Kuba people fell within the territory King Leopold supposedly controlled, but they were so far from the main routes along the Congo River that Leopold's forces had not yet ventured into their area.

The governmental structure of the Kuba kingdom was highly developed. An annual meeting in Ifuca drew all the chiefs and headman of the tribes and villages. They reported important statistics on births, deaths, and harvests and informed the king of any other important events that had taken place during the previous year. At the conclusion of his report, each man performed a ceremonial dance.

Courts, laws, and lawyers existed in Kuba society. A royal police force handled thefts and other crimes. The king had councilors to advise him, and in his council chambers, carved

Kuba Ancestral Figures, Lower Congo, c. 1915 *The most highly developed artistic culture evolved in the lower Congo villages. These ancestral figures were done by the Kuba, a people whom the Belgian colonial regime had absorbed by 1910. The Kuba, a cluster of about 16 Bantu-speaking groups, were ruled by chiefs, with the overall chief, or king, holding his authority by divine right. Kuba art dealt with human themes; dolls or statues were created representative of the Kuba royal court.*

statues of former great kings were displayed. These statues were but one example of the high-quality art produced by the Kuba people. Indeed, many consider the Kuba to be among Africa's greatest artists. Along with their sculptures, Kuba masks, textiles, and carved furniture and tools find places in the world's finest museums. Anything that could be embellished,

Kuba Queen, c. 1920 *The Kuba were united as a kingdom about 1600. They live between the Kasai and Sankuru Rivers in southeastern Congo. The ruling group, the Bushongo, provides the overall chief or king. This is a photograph of the 85-year old widow of a Bushongo king.*

Spiritual Kuba Woman, c. 1915 *The Kuba attached spiritual meaning to many natural occurrences. For example, a local hot or boiling spring was credited with miraculous healing powers. Such springs have water temperatures substantially higher than air temperature of the surrounding area. This is a photograph of "the wife of the spirit of the boiling spring."*

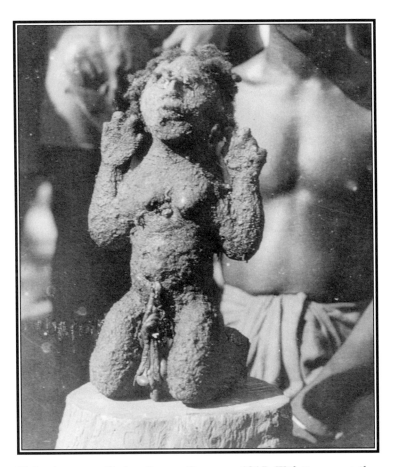

Kuba Ancestor Statue, Lower Congo, c. 1915 *With its many tribu-taries, the Congo River forms Africa's largest network of navigable waterways. It was only in the early years of the eighteenth century that the river was first called "Rio Congo," a name taken from the kingdom of the Kongo that had been located on the lower part of the river's course.*

The human figure is used by the peoples of the lower Congo in the decoration of almost every work—from ceremonial objects and domestic utensils to pieces of furniture and architectural design. A majority of the carved figures are made of wood, although some metal and ivory work has been found. Some of the figures, especially those in metal, show the influence of the Portuguese missionaries. Ancestor figures, such as the one in this photograph, are more realistically expressive than the artwork of other Congo areas.

from cups to knives, was carved. Their textiles feature brilliant colors and elaborate beadwork.

The Kuba believed in Chembe, an all-knowing, divine creator who still controlled nature but whose acts were not always understandable to mortals. The Kuba believed that if they implored Chembe, he would influence certain events, such as the success of a hunt or the fertility of Kuba women. But if they did not honor Chembe by following proper ceremonies or if they did something to belittle him, the Kuba were convinced that Chembe could send disaster. In addition to Chembe, the Kuba believed in the spirits of nature.

The Kuba creation story told of the first man and first woman being let down from the skies by a rope. When they landed on earth, they untied themselves and the rope drew back up into heaven.

When a person of stature in the Kuba community died, the slaves of that person were often killed as well so that they could continue to provide service to the deceased in the afterlife.

William Sheppard feared he was about to discover just how close he was to the afterlife when he spotted Toen-zaide returning from the capital. Fortunately the news was good. The king and his councilors had decided that the only explanation for the stranger knowing their language, combined with the fact that he was dark-skinned, was that he was a reincarnated spirit. Toen-zaide relayed to Sheppard the news that he was Bope Mekabe, a former king. Although Sheppard did not know it, the name Bope Mekabe does not appear in the Kuba royal genealogy. Anthropologist Jan Vansina has theorized that the Kuba may have known very well who Sheppard was but were simply trying to flatter him and get him to reveal other European plans to enter the kingdom.

In any event, Sheppard protested that he was not Bope Mekabe, but the representative of a king greater than any king on earth. No one listened to him. He was taken to the capital with great fanfare, and while traveling, he estimated that the city of Ifuca had about 5,000 citizens. Sheppard was told that a formal reception in his honor would take place in four days, after

Kuba Fortune Teller, c. 1920 *This man is divining, or prophesying, the future using a gourd filled with white chalk. The Kuba religion is dominated by nature spirits, the spirits of dead kings, and witchcraft. Nearly all objects of daily use are decorated. Carved wooden figurines, masks, and beautifully embroidered hand-woven raffia cloth are especially prized export items.*

Kuba Basket Weaver, c. 1920 *Kuba art is one of the most highly developed of all African traditions. It is a significant part of the Kuba cultural heritage. According to legend, their 27th king invented fire and was the first to make clothing using bark cloth—and the first to weave baskets. Kuba metalwork—in which one metal often was inlaid with another—used copper, iron, and brass. Their weapons and tools were crafted both to be used and to be admired.*

sufficient preparations had taken place. In the meantime, he was installed in a fine residence, befitting a person of high rank.

The missionary took careful notes of everything he saw that first week in Ifuca and throughout his four-month stay in the capital city. These notes became an important source of information about Kuba civilization before it was changed by Europeans.

On the day of the formal reception, Sheppard was led to a large square planted with beautiful trees. The area was surrounded by cloth hangings, designed and woven by the Kuba. The king's approximately 700 wives sat in a reserved area. Near them sat the king's sister. Suddenly the people stood and shouted. Kot aMbweeky II appeared, carried on the royal hammock by 18 attendants. He was about 70 to 75 years old and wore "a blue savalese cloth trimmed with beads and cowries, a blue and white beaded crown with a white tassel in it, and small brass rings, the sign of royalty, around his neck and legs," Sheppard reported.

As music played, the attendants lowered their king onto leopard skins and blankets. His subjects treated him as a deity. They lay face down in front of him. If the king sneezed, they sneezed. If he coughed, they coughed. And at the end of every sentence he spoke, they clapped in unison.

Kot aMbweeky II greeted Sheppard as a relative. He gave the missionary a knife that had been in the royal family for seven generations. When Sheppard asked, the king gave permission for him to preach to his people, as long as no one—including Sheppard—tried to leave the city without the king's permission.

The Kuba listened politely to everything Sheppard told them about the "Great King," but no one turned to Christianity. They were perfectly content with their lives and beliefs and saw no reason to change. Four months later, William Sheppard sought permission to leave because he needed to visit England and the United States. The king agreed on a one-year absence, to be measured by tying knots at each full moon. He also insisted that the missionary leave two of his own men in the capital as a guarantee of his return.

Sheppard would never see Kot aMbweeky II again. During his absence, the king died. After some internal conflict, he was replaced by a nephew. The nephew and his successors, while

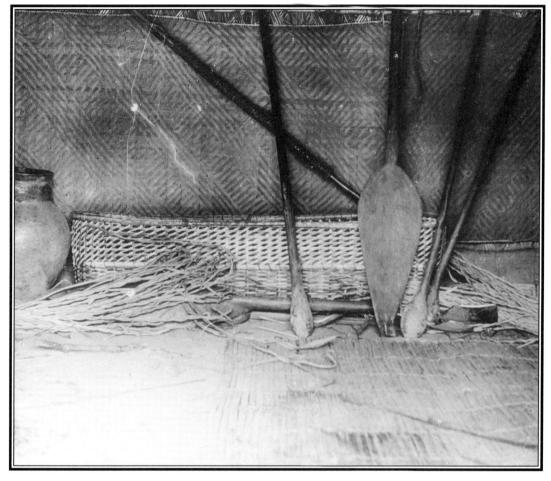

Kuba Raffia Cloth, c. 1920 *The Kuba women are noted for their embroidering of raffia cloth. Often dyed, this raffia is woven into complicated geometric patterns.*

not openly hostile, held Sheppard and his missionary friends at arm's length because of their friendship with Kot aMbweeky II, but Sheppard never lost hope that he would be able to spread Christianity among the Kuba people.

In 1900 disaster struck the Kuba capital. A rich concentration of rubber vines grew along the Kasai River that bordered the Kuba kingdom. Needing new sources of rubber, King

Leopold's forces attacked and looted Ifuca to ensure a docile population who could be forced to harvest the rubber. The outlying villages were quickly overwhelmed. At that moment, William Sheppard's ministry expanded. He would speak to the world about how the Kuba were treated and do everything in his power to bring the abuse to an end.

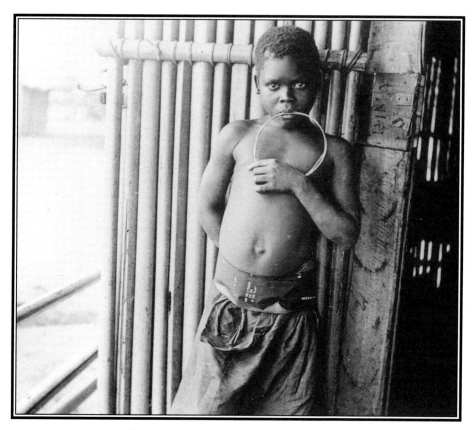

Congo Boy, c. 1908 *Émil Torday photographed this boy somewhere in the central Congo. Note the railroad track to the left. Undoubtedly, the track was part of the Matadi-Kinshasa Railway, which began operating in 1898. In 1892 Belgian authorities realized that the central Congo had an abundance of copal, a substance used in making varnish and printing ink. Almost immediately, orders were given to collect copal by whatever means necessary. Using the coercive threat of violence, Congo copal exports rose dramatically, especially with the completion of the Matadi-Kinshasa Railway. Between 1903 and 1906 exports more than doubled, a rise that helped compensate European investors for the loss of revenue resulting from the progressive destruction of rubber vines in this area.*

7

MURDER
INCORPORATED

The ease with which the Kuba were subdued in 1900 had its roots in the events of 1888. During that year King Leopold organized the groups of African mercenaries he'd been using to control the Congo Free State. He called his new army the Force Publique and placed African soldiers under white officers. During the next 12 years, the army grew to more than 19,000 members. Its job was threefold: to act as a police force, to guarantee that the Congolese submitted to their European masters' demands, and to fight guerrilla groups seeking freedom.

The Force Publique reinforced the orders of state officers King Leopold appointed to assist the governor-general in overseeing the Congo Free State. His colony covered roughly 1 million square miles, and the river and its tributaries made up more than 7,000 miles of interconnecting waterways. The king divided the territory into 14 districts, each divided into zones. The zones were further divided, and all these units were headed by Leopold-chosen white men.

These appointees made sure that Africans harvested palm nut oil, timber, and ivory. Under the terms of the hundreds of treaties signed by chiefs during the previous decade, Africans were required to collect the raw materials and received little, if any, pay. When local villages objected, small garrisons of the Force Publique forced people to obey. Their repeating rifles could fire a dozen or more shots without being reloaded. They also made frequent use of the *chicotte,* a long whip made from hippopotamus hide. Four African soldiers would hold an offender, face down, on the ground. Another African soldier, using the whip, lashed the person's back, buttocks, and legs anywhere from 25 to 100 times, ripping the flesh open. Few people survived a 100-lash beating with the *chicotte.*

Tens of thousands of Africans were also forced to act as porters, carrying tons of equipment, food, and ammunition over the Crystal Mountains to Stanley Pool. Steamboats were dismantled and portaged around the 200 miles of rapids, then reassembled and used to transport people, supplies, and raw materials up and down the remainder of the Congo River. Often the porters were chained, making the work more difficult. If they didn't move quickly enough, they were whipped. Some were tied to stakes and left in the sun to die. Villages became deserted as people fled into the rain forest, trying to escape the dangerous work and brutal treatment.

Africans were also targets of such treatment during construction of the railroad around the rapids, a project that took 11 years to complete. Surveying began in 1887. Deep ravines meant that any worker was only one misstep from instant death. When the surveying was completed in 1890, more Africans were forced to construct the narrow-gauge railroad. The human cost was incalculable. Tropical diseases killed both white and black men. The food was bad, and floggings with the *chicotte* increased. Freight cars of dynamite accidentally exploded, blowing workers to bits. While the European workers could cancel their contracts and go home, the Africans had no such option.

Local legend says that each tie on the railway line cost one African life, while each telegraph pole cost one European life. Official figures put the railway death toll at 132 whites and 1,800 nonwhites. Experts believe that in reality, 1,800 whites died during just the first two years and that the number of nonwhites who died was significantly higher.

In 1890 a young Polish man named Józef Konrad Korzeniowski went to the Congo to serve as an apprentice steamboat officer. He arrived at the Congo in a ship holding the first rails and ties for the railway. Korzeniowski was full of idealism and believed King Leopold's claims of a noble mission to Central Africa. But the man whom the world later came to know as Joseph Conrad was quickly disillusioned. During his six months in the Congo, he witnessed brutality that changed his view of humanity. Eight years later, he wrote the novel *Heart of Darkness*, which he said was "experience . . . pushed a little (and only very little) beyond the actual facts of the case."

The railroad was completed in 1898, and a ceremony was held at Stanley Pool. Adam Hochschild points out one of the great ironies of that event in *King Leopold's Ghost,* his study of the Congo Free State: "Officials erected a monument on the old caravan route that the rail line had replaced: three life-size metal figures of porters—one carrying a large box on his head, two collapsed in exhaustion beside him. The inscription read: THE RAILWAY FREED THEM FROM PORTERAGE. It said nothing about who made them become porters in the first place."

Children were not protected from the dangers of working for King Leopold. Seven- to nine-year-old boys and girls carried 22-pound loads up steep, treacherous paths. In 1890, at the same time Joseph Conrad was discovering the Congo, King Leopold determined that three children's colonies should be established. "The aim of these colonies is above all to furnish us with soldiers," he wrote on April 27. In response to the king's order, the governor-general of the Congo Free State commanded district commissioners to gather as many boys as possible.

These colonies and similar colonies that were established over the following years were run by both the state and Roman Catholic missionaries from Belgium. King Leopold donated large sums of money to the Catholic Church in Belgium, and the missionaries were dependent on his continued support. The children taken were labeled orphans, but they had no need for another home. African societies had a strong sense of the extended family, and children who were orphaned were adopted by the larger family or clan to which they belonged. Some of the children weren't orphans at all.

Conditions in the children's colonies were atrocious. The children were controlled with the *chicotte*. Disease was common, and the death rate often exceeded 50 percent. Thousands of children never made it to the colonies. During 1892–93, a group of 108 boys was forced to march to the state colony at Boma. Only 62 boys survived the journey, and eight of those died shortly after their arrival.

King Leopold was a master at distancing himself from such horrors. He gave orders about how much raw material the Congo should produce but never questioned how those quotas were reached. He gave private companies control over various areas of the Congo Free State to ease the drain on his finances. What wasn't made public was that Leopold was half-owner of most of those companies, so he received half of their profits plus other fees. He never once set foot in the Congo Free State.

Eastern Congo was largely controlled by Tippu Tip, an African Arabian who had made his fortune in ivory and the slave trade and had helped Henry Stanley during some of his expeditions. In 1887 Leopold invited Tippu Tip to be governor of the Congo's eastern province. The slave trader agreed. This spared the king the necessity of trying to unseat a strong local leader, and it gave Tippu Tip access to the west by way of the Congo River. The arrangement worked for a few years. But there were problems on both sides. Tippu Tip's men never appreciated taking orders from Leopold's European commissioners. King Leopold was criticized for his relationship with one of the region's most notorious slave traders. He also thought Tippu Tip's forces were competing with him for ivory. The relationship eventually had to fail.

King Leopold announced to Europe that he was going to drive out the "evil slave traders" from the East Congo. The resulting war was brutal with accounts of cannibalism on both sides. Since the Europeans and their African troops had greater firepower, the war ended with victory for Leopold in early 1894. Having established his authority in the region, the king quietly returned many of the slave traders to their previous positions in the Congo government.

It was also during the 1890s that rubber became much more important to King Leopold. A worldwide rubber boom broke out as industry began to understand the many uses for this natural substance. The equatorial African rain forest, which ran through nearly half of the Congo, was full of wild rubber vines. Yet profits from wild rubber would not last forever. Rubber trees were being cultivated in plantations in Latin America and Asia; although those trees would not be mature for years, when they were ready to be harvested the price of rubber would plummet. The king was determined to gather every drop of rubber from the Congo before that happened.

Harvesting rubber was a laborious process. Rubber is coagulated sap from specific vines and trees. In the Congo it came from a long, spongy vine that was up to a foot thick at the base and climbed as much as 100 feet up a tree to reach sunlight. Once there, the vine would spread hundreds of more feet through the upper limbs of other trees. To collect rubber, a worker cut the vine with a knife. Sap slowly dripped from the cut. Workers hung buckets and earthen pots to catch the milky sap. It had the consistency of syrup.

When the vines near the ground were tapped dry, workers climbed the trees to get at the sap that was higher up. Sometimes they would fall, either killing themselves or breaking their backs. Before long, the vines surrounding a village would be tapped dry. Workers would travel farther into the forest, often traveling two or more days to reach fresh vines. They were supposed to make only small cuts in the vines, but as demand increased, most workers resorted to cutting the vines completely in half. This method increased the amount of rubber they could harvest, but it also killed the plant.

Once the sap was collected, it had to dry so that it would coagulate. Often the only way to accomplish this was for the worker to spread the sap over his arms, thighs, and chest.

Pulling the coagulated sap off was extremely painful, because body hair would stick to the sap.

Understandably, no one wanted to harvest rubber, but the Force Publique enforced requirements for rubber collection. Sporadic rebellions against this forced labor became more frequent as the quotas for rubber increased. Even units of the Force Publique began to mutiny. Sometimes this was in protest of how other Africans were being treated. Other times soldiers were demanding a greater share of the profits. European officers in the Force Publique responded to these rebellions by increasing the beatings, hangings, and arbitrary executions. They held women and children of villages hostage until the men had harvested the required amount of rubber. The hostages were crammed into stockades, where they received little food, and sometimes soldiers unchained and raped the women.

If a village refused to cooperate, the Force Publique would often kill everyone as an example to neighboring villages. Fearful that African soldiers might save their ammunition for a future mutiny, some white officers required soldiers to prove that every bullet used had actually killed someone. Adapting a practice of African slave traders, the officers usually demanded the severed right hand from a corpse. Because it might take days for soldiers to return to their garrisons, baskets of hands were smoked to keep them from decaying before being counted. Officers often told their soldiers that they would be released from service more quickly if they turned in more hands, so some soldiers amputated the hands of the living.

Throughout the 1890s missionaries such as William Sheppard told the outside world of this brutality. King Leopold used his public relations skills and his humanitarian reputation to deny the stories. He also kept as many questioning foreigners out of the Congo as possible.

Then, in 1895, a Congo state officer killed a white man. Europeans wondered if state officers would kill a white man, what they might do to Africans. To allay European suspicions, Leopold quickly established the Commission for the Protection of the Natives. Made up of three Belgian Catholic missionaries and three foreign Protestants, the commission was a public relations coup. Leopold was lauded throughout Europe. In reality the commission was a sham. Its members were separated by thousands of miles and had no power to change things.

As the century closed, Leopold was satisfied that he controlled the Congo and how it was perceived. What he did not suspect was that a major threat to his power lay in the hands of a 28-year-old English shipping clerk. Edmund Dene Morel was ideally positioned to make three astonishing discoveries that would revolutionize how the world viewed the Belgian king.

Wangilima Cone Huts, 1910 *In 1910 Robert L. Reid mapped the Aruwimi River, a tributary of the Congo. This river became important in the European trade with the native population—western merchandise for rubber and ivory. Reid described the Wangilima people who lived along the river as prosperous, peaceful, and very knowledgeable about the jagged rock masses and river rapids.*

The Wangilima villages were close to the river, built on clay banks. The high cone huts, seven to eight feet across and about fifteen feet tall, stood on small sticks, driven closely together into the ground. The interior hut floor was a raised foot of earth. The outside walls were covered with three or four layers of large leaves laid like scales of a fish and sewn on with cane. The top of the cone was finished off with an old pot or round pleated basketwork stuck together with several skewers, like large hat pins.

8

CAMPAIGN OF
CONVICTIONS

Edmund Dene Morel was the last person anyone would suspect of being able to cause King Leopold trouble. Responsible for his widowed mother, his wife, and a growing number of children, Morel worked hard for Elder Dempster, a large British company whose ships were contracted to carry all cargo between Europe and the Congo Free State. To supplement his income, Morel wrote magazine and newspaper articles about African trade issues. He was a careful researcher who was known for his solidly probusiness attitudes, and he had praised King Leopold's policies in the Congo.

Morel spent much of his childhood in France, so he was fluent in both English and French. This made him the ideal man in the company to keep track of cargo coming and going from Antwerp, Belgium, where French was the official language. Because of his hard work, he received a series of promotions and became the company's liaison with officials of the Congo state who worked from Belgium.

A meeting with one of these men, the secretary of state for the Congo Free State, first awakened Morel's suspicions. The official complained that "confidential information" about cargo had been passed on to the press. He pointed out a specific paragraph that seemed innocent enough to Morel. It described the main items being shipped to the Congo in the latest steamer. The list included ammunition and military muskets.

"That is the fault," Morel later recorded. "That is the lapse from professional secrecy. As the enormity of the indiscretion is denounced, the speaker rises, the cadaverous cheeks flush, the voice trembles . . . the long bony fingers saw the air. He will hear no excuses; allow no interruption. . . . The youngest individual present leaves the room wondering why so large a quantity of material of war is required . . . why its export should be kept secret and why the Congo Government should be so greatly troubled at the 'indiscretion.'"

By making such a major issue of what seemed to Morel to be a minor infraction, the official roused Morel's mistrust. He compared the records of shipments that he kept for Elder Dempster with the figures being released to the public by the Congo Free State. The figures did not match. He looked at the figures more carefully. Three disturbing facts became clear to him. First, the arms shipment whose public announcement had so upset the Congo official was not an isolated incident. For at least the past few years, huge quantities of arms had been regularly shipped to either the Congo Free State itself or to one of the trading companies the king had working inside the Congo. "To what usage was this armament put?" the young clerk asked himself.

Second, the value of the cargoes received in Antwerp was many times larger than that reported in the public trade statistics. Someone was taking what today would equal tens of millions of dollars off the top. Business in the Congo was much more lucrative than King Leopold had led the world to believe. "Into whose pocket did the unavowed surplus go?" Morel asked.

Third, Morel determined that about 80 percent of the cargo being sent to the Congo had nothing to do with trade. It could not be used to pay Africans for work they were doing for the state. Knowing the worth of the rubber and ivory being taken out of the Congo and realizing that Elder Dempster's exclusive contract meant cargo couldn't be entering the Congo from other sources, Morel reached a disturbing conclusion: "Nothing was going in to pay for what was coming out."

Suddenly he understood the arms shipments. The Congo Free State was maintaining a small army and using slave labor to cut costs. He wrote: "Forced labour of a terrible and continuous kind could alone explain such unheard-of profits . . . forced labour in which the Congo Government was the immediate beneficiary; forced labour directed by the closest associates of the King himself. . . . It must be bad enough to stumble upon a murder. I had stumbled upon a secret society of murderers with a King for a croniman."

The first thing Morel did was to speak with his boss, Sir Alfred Jones. The next day, Sir Alfred traveled to Belgium and met with the king. He returned to Liverpool with assurances that reforms were being made. They just needed time. Morel was not convinced. But he also sensed that his employers were not happy with the possibility that he might make his knowledge public, thereby putting at risk one of their largest shipping contracts. First they offered him a pay raise—with a transfer to another country. Then his boss offered him a thinly veiled bribe. Morel rejected both offers.

In 1900 the young man wrote a series of anonymous articles about "The Congo Scandal," which appeared in the *Speaker*. They created a sensation in England, as well as at Elder Dempster. Knowing that his concerns were on a collision course with the business interests of his employer, the next year Morel quit his job and began a full-time journalistic crusade to expose and destroy Leopold's reign of terror. For the first time, a critic of the Belgian king had access to hard figures. He also had a gift for publicity.

Defenders of Leopold were genuinely puzzled as to why Morel would risk everything to expose events in the Congo. He wasn't rich, and he had a family to support, yet he turned his back on a promising career. He also wasn't driven by religious convictions. His friendship with anthropologist Mary Kingsley convinced him that African culture was being destroyed by outside influences, particularly by missionaries. His own words attribute his motivation simply to being the person he was: "To have sat still . . . would have been temperamentally impossible," he wrote.

Adding to his motivation was the unswerving support of his wife, Mary Florence Richardson. Married in 1896, the couple had five children. Morel's peers frequently praised the influence and integrity of his wife. Morel dedicated his book *Great Britain and the Congo,* published in 1909, "to her whose steadfast courage and unswerving faith have made it possible." This opinion of his wife hadn't changed nine years later when he told René Claparède, "I should never have done what I have without my wife's help. I was often discouraged. It was she who invariably made me strong again by saying to me, 'Go on.'" His friend John Holt said, "I always think of her as part of you, the two constituting the Morel of Congo reform."

When he severed his ties with Elder Dempster, Edmund Morel became a man on a mission. He wrote articles and pamphlets, full of the same painstaking research that had built his journalistic career. While privately he did not support the missionary movement in Africa—"They [the Baptist Missionary Society] are a cowardly, dishonest crowd," he wrote to a friend, "though you need not pass this on!"—he understood that the involvement of missionaries and other church leaders was essential to the success of his work.

As Morel's campaign spread from England to the European continent and to America, he was joined by political and religious leaders from all over. Current and former employees at Elder Dempster and at various companies in the Congo passed on incriminating evidence to Morel. He used it to further incense the public. On May 20, 1903, the British House of Commons unanimously passed a Congo protest resolution asking the government to confer with the other nations who had signed the Berlin agreement in 1885 so that measures could be taken to "abate the evils prevalent in that State."

Meanwhile, Roger Casement, the British consul in the Congo, was ordered to investigate the claims of atrocities in the interior of the Congo and to report back as soon as possible. He spent three months investigating and was increasingly appalled by what he saw. Highly populated villages he had seen in 1887 now stood deserted. He quickly learned that the sight of any white man caused people to flee into the forest, carrying everything they could with them. His anger built. By August 30, 1903, he was writing in his diary, "16 men women and children tied up from a village . . . close to the town. Infamous. The men were put in the prison, the children let go at my intervention. Infamous. Infamous, shameful system."

His initial reports led the Foreign Office to recall him to England, where he prepared a formal report. It included documents given to him by the Reverend John Whitehead, a misionary still working in the Congo, as well as detailed accounts of incidents that Casement had personally seen or been told of by witnesses. Typical of the report was this account of a 12-year-old boy who had lost his right hand when he was about seven years old:

> The soldiers had come . . . by land through the forest. They were led by an officer whose name was given as U. V. His father and mother were killed beside him. He saw them killed, and a bullet hit him and he fell. He then showed me a deep cicatrized scar at the back of the head, just at the nape of the neck, and said it was there the bullet had struck him. He fell down, presumably insensible, but came to his senses while his hand was being hacked off at the wrist. I asked him how it was he could possibly lie silent and give no sign. He answered that he felt the cutting, but was afraid to move, knowing that he would be killed, if he showed any sign of life.

The report went on for 39 pages, with an additional 23-page appendix. When it was released in February 1904, it shocked the world. Casement's report confirmed and expanded on every charge made by Morel and his associates.

Morel seized the opportunity. By March 23, he was ready to announce the formation of the Congo Reform Association. "The Congo evil has grown to colossal dimensions," stated the first release of the organization, "and it can only be put an end to by an organized public opinion which shall insist upon the rulers of civilized mankind terminating a wrong which has been allowed to reach its present state in private, but which to-day constitutes a public affront to humanity." Soon many prominent members of the British Parliament and churches had joined the work.

King Leopold recognized the danger he faced. He told local officials to hold a "judicial enquiry," a move that was dismissed by the British as superficial. Then he appointed a Commission of Enquiry to go to the Congo and formally investigate all charges. He intended this committee to whitewash the brutalities, but his tactics backfired. The committee members were horrified by what they witnessed, and their report substantiated Morel's and Casement's charges. Further, their conclusions could not be dismissed as part of a personal vendetta. They had been sent to the Congo by the king himself.

The report was scheduled for release on November 3, 1905. Seeking to control damage, the king arranged for all press offices to receive a summary of the report the day before. It was allegedly sent out by the West African Missionary Association, a dummy corporation, when in reality the summary had been delivered to England by a Belgian priest whose church had just received a large donation from Leopold. The summary grossly distorted the commission's findings.

Anticipating this action, Morel had written to every missionary in the Congo with whom he had contact and asked them to send him copies of the depositions they made before the commission. The Congo Reform Association quickly published what the missionaries sent. By 1906 Morel had published two books that further inflamed public opinion: *King Leopold's Rule in Africa* and *Red Rubber: The Story of the Rubber Slave Trade Flourishing on the Congo in the Year of Grace 1906*. His public presentations featured a 60-photo slide show that included six shots of mutilated Africans. These slides were also made available to the press. Millions of people were exposed to them.

In spite of Leopold's best efforts to control world opinion, the evidence was too great to ignore. By the end of 1906, governments in the United States and Europe had reached a consensus: it was time to take the Congo away from the king.

Tribal Chief, Eastern Congo, 1906 *This tribal chief is photographed "in his easy chair." Recently the Congo government established Maiko National Park, some 4,000 square miles in the eastern part of the country. Gorillas, elephants, leopards, chimpanzees, and aardvarks dwell in the park, which has not yet been opened for tourists.*

9

THE BIRTH OF THE BELGIAN CONGO

King Leopold was cornered. The public relations campaign mounted by the Congo Reform Association, aided by missionaries returning to Europe who brought *chicottes,* shackles, photos, and horrifying stories, had thoroughly destroyed his reputation. The one Englishman he could count on to defend him, Henry M. Stanley, had died in 1904, shortly after the release of the Casement report.

Other attempts to counter the bad publicity backfired. In December 1906 a disenchanted former lobbyist for the king sold newspaper magnate William Randolph Hearst documents detailing the king's attempts to influence the U.S. Congress and bribe both officials and journalists to keep quiet. Hearst splashed the story across the front page of his papers every day for a week, complete with graphic photos of the atrocities taking place in the Congo. In Belgium the king was not popular either. People were scandalized that their monarch, a man in his 70s, was having an open affair with a 16-year-old prostitute.

Leopold fell back on his political skills. He knew western leaders wanted Belgium to take over his colony and that the Belgian government was feeling increasing pressure to take action. British activists were organizing a boycott of Portuguese products because of the use of forced labor in its African colonies. If Belgian political leaders didn't act quickly, Belgium might face a similar boycott, bringing economic disaster to the small country. A more powerful country might take over the colony as well.

Leopold used that pressure to his advantage. If he was forced to give up his colony, he'd make Belgium pay dearly. Negotiations dragged on for more than a year. Leopold refused to give the government accounts of the Congo Free State's finances. He threw temper tantrums. Using one delaying tactic after another, he gave himself time to hide the wealth he had gained from his colony. Finally an agreement was reached. In December 1907 Jules de Trooz, prime minister of Belgium, announced the proposed terms for the Belgian takeover of the Congo. Called the Treaty of Cession, it said nothing about initiating reforms. It simply stated that Belgium would take over the debts of the Congo Free State and that Leopold would remain a partner in the Congo companies.

An immediate outcry rose up in Belgium. Socialists, Liberals, and Catholics decided to fight the prime minister. His party soon lost majority control of the government, and on December 31, 1907, the prime minister collapsed and died. The new government was led by Franz Schollaert.

Equally outraged were reformers in both Britain and the United States. On January 23, 1908, the two nations jointly insisted that Schollaert's government recognize its responsibility to follow the guarantees in the Berlin and Brussels Acts to respect "freedom of trade, rights of missionaries, and humane treatment of natives."

Schoellert was in a precarious position. His new government had a tenuous hold on power. The people of Belgium were deeply divided over what should be done. And now he needed to compel a stubborn old king to give in to two foreign powers. Within a week he came up with a proposal that Leopold agreed to. The king would give up his place in the Congo companies, but Belgium would take over the responsibilities for the Congo Free State's many loans (including those it had made to the king), complete the public works projects the king had been funding, and pay him an annual stipend for the "sacrifices" he had made. That money would come from the Congolese.

The Belgian Parliament debated the treaty, and after adding a provision that made the colony subject to the Belgian government, the Treaty of Cession passed. Leopold signed it into law on October 18,1908. The agreement did not guarantee reforms, a measure insisted on by both Britain and the United States. Leopold suggested that Belgium simply not ask those two nations for recognition of the new colony. The government followed his advice. In effect, conditions in the Congo had not changed.

When British Foreign Minister Sir Edward Grey discovered what had been done, he decided to ask the nations that had signed the Berlin Act to unite in opposition to the Treaty of Cession. Much to his amazement, only the United States joined Britain in refusing to recognize the Belgian Congo. France gave its recognition in exchange for settling border disputes and other issues. Germany chose the same route. Other European nations failed to understand why Britain and the United States were so upset. Colonial powers had been exploiting their colonies for centuries.

Meanwhile, a situation in the Kasai River valley was about to draw international attention to the Congo once again. African-American missionary William Sheppard had continued working with the Kuba people. His efforts to assist them were supported by his boss, William Morrison, who headed the Southern Presbyterian Congo mission. After the Force Publique had overtaken the Kuba kingdom, the company in control of the region had discovered that the Kasai River valley was the most lucrative source of rubber in the Congo. The Compagnie du Kasai (CK) was brutal in its efforts to get all the rubber extracted.

Some Kuba revolted, given assurances from their elders that a fetish would change the white man's bullets into water. The fetish did not work, and 180 Kuba were killed. Sheppard wrote about the horrid changes in Kuba life for the *Kasai Herald,* an

Typical Village, Katanga Area, 1907 *This photograph was taken by British naturalist S.A. Neave, who spent more than two years in the Katanga area of the Congo (1906–1909). Many of these native villages in the Katanga were destroyed by Belgian colonial authorities. This copper-producing area forced labor, the construction of roads, smelters, mining towns, and the ravaging of villages. A Belgian minister wrote in 1916, "It is necessary to engage the population in work, oblige them to produce and accumulate, and lead them by the hand. . .[Compulsory labor] will raise the native outside of his barbarism and give him the economic notions and activities that he misses today."*

The Belgian exploitation of Katanga led to the destruction of traditional village life. The advent of poverty undermined the social structure and resulted in third-world status.

annual publication for Presbyterian mission supporters in America. He started by describing the way of life he had originally discovered among the Kuba:

These great stalwart men and women, who have from time immemorial been free, cultivating large crops of Indian corn, tobacco, potatoes, trapping elephants for their ivory and leopards for their skins, who have always had their own king and a government not to be despised, officers of the law, established in every town of the kingdom; these magnificent people, perhaps about 400,000 in number, have entered a new chapter in the history of their tribe. Only a few years since travelers through this country found them living in large homes, having from one to four rooms in each house, loving and living happily with their wives and children, one of the most prosperous and intelligent of all the African tribes, though living in one of the most remote spots on the planet. . . .

But within these last three years how changed they are! Their farms are growing up in weeds and jungle, their king is practically a slave, their houses now are mostly only half-built single rooms, and are much neglected. The streets of their towns are not clean and well-swept as they once were. Even their children cry for bread.

Why this change? You have it in a few words. There are armed sentries of chartered trading companies, who force the men and women to spend most of their days and nights in the forests making rubber, and the price they receive is so meager that they cannot live upon it. In the majority of the villages these people have not time to listen to the gospel story, or give an answer concerning their soul's salvation. Looking upon the changed scene now, one can only join with them in their groans as they must say: "Our burdens are greater than we can bear."

The Compagnie du Kasai was outraged by this description. Matters grew worse from the company's perspective when the British vice consul to the Congo, Wilfred Thesiger, spent three months personally investigating conditions in the Kasai basin. Presbyterian missionaries, including William Sheppard, assisted him. Thesiger submitted a scathing report to the British Parliament. The price of Compagnie du Kasai stock went into a free fall.

Company members knew they had no legal grounds to punish the Presbyterians for the help they had given Thesiger. But they could get at both Sheppard and Morrison, because technically the article for the *Kasai Herald* had been published in the Congo, which was illegal. In February 1909 the company filed suit against both men. Sheppard was accused of libel, and Morrison was charged because he had published the piece.

The two men wrote to supporters about the situation and decided to face prison rather than pay any fine that might be levied against them. World interest soon focused on the case. The American legation in Brussels told the Belgian government that U.S. recognition of Belgium's claim to the Congo might rest on how the case was decided. When the trial took place in Leopoldville on September 20, 1909, charges against Morrison were dropped on a technicality. This left only Sheppard accused. E. D. Morel had asked Émile Vandervelde, leader of the Belgian socialists, to recommend a lawyer. Vandervelde chose to travel to the Congo himself and serve in that function.

Two days after the trial, Morrison wrote to Morel, praising Vandervelde's representation. "[He] made a magnificent defence," Morel wrote. "His speech was a marvel of eloquence, invincible in logic, burning sarcasm and pathetic appeal for justice to be done in this case, not only for us missionaries, but especially for the native people."

Two weeks later, on October 4, 1909, the judge rendered his decision. He found Sheppard not guilty because "the defendant Sheppard did not have the evil intention to injure the plaintiff and that the article which appeared in the *Kasai Herald* of the 1st of January, 1908 did not contain accusations against it." The CK had to pay court costs.

That same month, the Belgian Parliament announced how reforms would take place in the Congo. Over the next three years, free trade would be phased in. Eventually Africans would be allowed to buy and sell rubber as they chose. Morel was incensed. "There has been a change of name, but the old firm remains and is carrying on the old game of plunder and slavery," he said. He attacked British Foreign Secretary Grey for not protesting, and the Congo Reform Association began splintering because of the conflict.

Completed Mining Camp House, Kambove, 1907 *These communal copper mining camp houses contributed to the destruction of traditional native living patterns in the Katanga region. European investment in Congo mining resulted in several independent monopolies receiving land and mineral concessions from Brussels while at the same time retaining close personal and financial links with the Belgian government.*

The mineral revolution—which World War I (1914–18) accelerated—created an obsession with the need for large-scale mining. An unprecedented number of Congolese natives were forced into the European-run economy. According to Belgian government statistics, native wage earners in the Congo increased from 45,000 in 1916 to 278,000 in 1924 and to 427,000 by 1927.

Two months later, on December 17, 1909, King Leopold II died, and his nephew Prince Albert became Belgium's new king, giving reformers new hope. However, the problems remained. Morel was quick to note that the Force Publique didn't even change its name, that the same men were station agents throughout the Congo, and that the new Belgian minister of colonies had earlier used thousands of forced laborers to build railways

Native Chief, Lufira River Area, c. 1907 *The Lufira River, which rises in the Katanga Plateau, is on the copper-rich area of southeastern Congo. Today a dam near the city of Likasi forms a 160-square-mile lake that provides water storage for a power station. This station generates electricity for the smelting industry of Likasi and the copper zone between the cities of the Kambove and Lubumbashi.*

King Leopold extended his military control over the Katanga area in the 1890s. A railroad was constructed to bypass the Congo River, which was navigable only by steamer. The brutal, unrestrained rule of Leopold virtually ended the traditional authority of village chiefs in the Katanga region. After independence from Belgium (1960), foreign mining interests encouraged Katanga to secede from the newly formed Congo nation. Political chaos and bloodshed followed. In 1963 Katanga gradually reintegrated with the Congo Republic, but unrest, especially over the profits from mining, continued throughout the rest of the twentieth century.

Mongo Huts Built for the Spirits of the Dead, 1905 *The Mongo include several ethnic groups living in the forest south of the main Congo River bend and north of the Kasai and Sankuru Rivers. Mongo religion placed strong emphasis on ancestor worship. They believed in many deities and spirits who were approachable only through the intervention of dead elders and relatives. Among the Mongo, in the mid-1930s, an anti-European cult called* Likili *arose in response to the lowering birthrate. According to collected oral history records, Mongo cult followers destroyed their western-style beds, mattresses, blankets, mosquito nets, and clothing in the belief that European goods had displeased the gods and thus caused the major birthrate decline.*

in the colony. Morel also worried that people would lose interest in the Congo now that the man they perceived as primarily responsible for its horrors—King Leopold— was dead.

At this key point in time, Morel gained an important ally: Sir Arthur Conan Doyle, the creator of Sherlock Holmes. Conan

Making a Fish Trap, Lake Kivu, 1906 *The British naturalist H.F.R. Wollaston spent more than two years (1905–06) in the highlands surrounding the Lake Kivu area of the eastern Congo. He was the first white person to enter many Congo villages in this region. As a naturalist, Wollaston was oblivious to the political scene that was dramatically affecting various Congo regions. Rather, he made many observations on other natural phenomena. He attributed the absence of crocodiles in Lake Kivu to the saltiness of the water, and he attempted to explain the horrors wrought by tick-fever and sleeping sickness. In 1914 the Royal Geographical Society awarded Wollaston its Gill Memorial Medal for "his exploring work in Central Africa."*

Lake Kivu is located between Congo to the west and Rwanda to the east. The lake's shores are densely populated. Fishing is the principal source of food for the inhabitants. Today Bukavu, the largest city on Lake Kivu, has an enormous overpopulation problem caused by hundreds of thousands of political refugees from the neighboring nations of Burundi and Rwanda.

Making Fire, Eastern Congo, 1906 *Fire is one of the human race's essential tools, control of which helped start it on the path toward civilization. Wollaston photographed this eastern Congo native making a fire by means of friction-producing implements.*

Doyle appeared throughout Great Britain, speaking against the evils still being perpetrated in the Congo. "So long as in any report of Congo reforms, such a sentence occurs as 'Adult natives will be compelled to work,'" he wrote in a letter to a newspaper, "there can be no true reform whatever."

Morel was encouraged by reports from missionaries that atrocities against rubber workers were dropping off. Missionaries and

"War Dance," Eastern Congo, 1906 *Wollaston described the peoples of the eastern Congo as peaceful and friendly. This dance, which he photographed and labeled as a "war dance" was undoubtedly a tribal dance or ritual ceremony performed to ensure the welfare of the land and the people. Generalizing about a tribal dance is difficult, as dances varied from one group to another. Usually, though, tribal dances are associated with some fertility or initiation rite, war, or hunting.*

British officials cited immense improvements in conditions. Many leaders within the Congo Reform Association began to feel that their job was done. In 1913 Britain recognized the Belgian Congo. Whatever his private misgivings, Morel realized it was time to declare victory. On June 16, 1913, the Congo Reform

Medicine Man, Central Congo, c. 1915 *In some cultures, "medicine men" are skilled in ritualistic healing of the sick and disabled—and in communicating with the world beyond. These people usually undergo a rigorous initiation rite to gain what others consider to be supernatural powers. The medicine men use various objects—such as feathers of a rare bird, odd-shaped stones, or hallucinogenic plants— to remove the sickness. Also, charms and potions are prepared to cure sickness or have some other magical effect. Often masks are worn having some social significance such as a fertility rite mask or one conveying religious symbolism. Because nonliterate societies frequently attributed illness to witches or sorcerers, eighteenth-century westerners coined the term "witch doctor" to describe a person who treats such conditions. Today this phase is considered pejorative.*

Association held its final meeting. "We have struck a blow for human justice that cannot and will not pass away," Morel stated.

Despite the fact that most of the atrocities ended, the Congolese still suffered. The Belgian Congo imposed taxes on each village, forcing people to work on plantations. No effort was

Medicine Man, Belgian Congo, 1915 *In the Congo, as in many other societies, medicine men are special people who can remove evil spirits, punish enemies, predict the weather, locate fish and game—and above all, heal the sick. Note the charms on this medicine man's arms and the chalk on his face. Such symbols were meant to convey supernatural power.*

made to give Africans citizenship or a voice in the Belgian government. It ruled its colony through what became known as "the Trinity": the colonial state apparatus, the Catholic Church, and private business.

Mining companies, desperate for workers because of the discontinuation of slavery, followed the South African model of hiring young men for short periods of time and then returning them to their homes. This disrupted village life, reduced the chief's authority, and drew criticism from missionaries and some field administrators. If a worker fled the mines, one of his family members would be put in prison—reminiscent of the hostage system.

Witnesses of life in the Congo between 1880 and 1920 and modern anthropologists who specialize in the Congo basin agree that about half the African population of the region died during that 40-year period. The population of the Belgian Congo in 1924 was estimated at 10 million. Based on that number, about 10 million people either died or were killed during King Leopold's reign and in the years immediately following the formation of the Belgian Congo. But the suffering of its people was not over.

Watusi Man and Woman, Near Goma, Lake Kivu, 1926 *The Watusi, or Tutsi, are tall people, averaging between six and seven and one-half feet. Chiefs administer local clans. Supreme control is held by a* mwami *("king") who must be from the Bega, the oldest Watusi branch. Spirits of deceased mwami are believed to dwell in leopards and continue to torment their people in that shape. Through the centuries, the Watusi dominated their Hutu neighbors. Unlike the agrarian Hutu, the Watusi considered work with a hoe demeaning. They made their living by owning and selling cattle. Belgian colonial administrators favored the Watusis, intensifying the animosity between these two peoples.*

Lake Kivu, one of the great lakes of East Africa, spans the boundary between Congo and Rwanda. Today the lake is part of the Virunga National Park, home to abundant wildlife including elephants, hippopotamuses, rare mountain gorillas, and antelopes. In 1994 UNESCO placed the park on the List of World Heritage Sites in danger because of the increasing number of permanent settlements within the park resulting from the great number of refugees fleeing the war in neighboring Rwanda. This photograph was taken by Elizabeth Ness (1880–1962), the first woman to become a Council member of the Royal Geographical Society. Mrs. Ness described her extensive travels in her autobiography, Ten Thousand Miles in Two Continents *(1929).*

10

THE HAUNTED REALM

As World War I ended, the "Trinity" continued to run life in the Belgian Congo. Mining companies, the largest representative of business interests, began looking for new answers to their labor problem. They developed a "manpower stabilization" policy that gave miners long-term, renewable contracts. By providing minimal housing, the companies encouraged families to move to the mines. This practice kept families together, but it removed them from their original villages. Of course, using Congolese workers saved the mines money. They paid African workers much less than whites.

The Belgian colonial government, the second part of the Trinity, wanted Africans to adopt European working styles. Mining and other private companies provided one means for accomplishing that goal. In 1917 the government also introduced agricultural programs in which Africans were required to raise crops rather than participate in traditional activities. Then, in the 1930s the government established farming settlements. Africans were resettled to areas where modern farming methods could be more easily introduced. These forced moves further weakened traditional ties.

During the first half of the twentieth century, the Congolese had no meaningful role in their government. Colonial administrators divided the Belgian Congo into arbitrary

Traditional Hut, c. 1915

Most Congolese lived in small villages that ranged in size from a few dozen to a few hundred people. The vast majority farmed small plots of land. They raised their own food, including cassava root, a source of tapioca, corn, and rice. Today few families can afford farm machinery, so most use hand tools. As a result, farm productivity is low, and most families are poor.

chiefdoms that rarely had any connection to traditional ethnic boundaries or political units. The administrators appointed chiefs, who were paid by the state to provide a link between the Belgian authorities and the Africans. Because the people were not allowed a role in selecting their chiefs or in making any other political decisions, two generations of Congolese had no experience in self-rule.

The Roman Catholic Church, the third part of the Trinity, was the primary provider of educational and vocational training. State subsidies covered almost the entire cost of Catholic missionaries working in the Belgian Congo. They portrayed Leopold as a hero.

Woman's Head, Lower Congo, c. 1915 *Before the European invasion, most of the Congo population lived in rural societies with strong traditions. The various groups were organized on a kinship basis. For example, the group who received a bride had to pay some material compensation to the group who had raised her. Known as* bridewealth, *this payment often was a symbolic as well as an economic exchange. It was a pledge that the wife would be well treated and it also was a compensation for her loss. Polygamy, in varying degrees, was common throughout the Congo.*

The system of running the Belgian Congo through the close cooperation of business, colonial administration, and the Catholic Church was not questioned until after World War II. The war effort increased the number of Africans moving to large towns. A new class of educated, French-speaking Africans began demanding reforms. Labor disputes and strikes in

Three Women, South Kosongo Area, c. 1920 *These South Kosongo women, living near Lake Tanganyika, adapted their hair dress to accommodate water carrying. Throughout the Congo, women, occupied a lower social status than men. Although economically incorporated into her husband's family, women had virtually no say in larger issues concerning the community. Generally, women did not own property. They received harsher penalties than men for social infractions like adultery.*

In 1885 Lever Brothers, predecessor of Unilever, was founded in Great Britain for the making and selling of soap. At first these wrapped bars were made from tallow and vegetable oils. In 1911 the company signed an agreement with Belgian Congo officials to develop palm tree plantations. The palm oil would be used as an ingredient in soap. Within 15 years, the area chosen by Lever for their palm fruit monopoly expanded into more than 4,500 square miles scattered throughout the Congo. A doctor from one of these Lever plantations described the impact on women:

> *The woman is suppose to remove the fruit from the hard fibrous parts [of the palm], which is considerable work, and then carry a basket weighing 20 to 30 kilograms [44–66 pounds] to the company post. . .To these tasks already mentioned and themselves hard, sometimes going beyond human possibility, there is also a daily walk of 10 to 30 kilometers [6–18 miles], half of it, with a heavy basket on the head. . . . We see old women deformed by illness, women with children on their backs, pregnant women, and pre-adolescent girls aging prematurely.*

the mining centers underscored the changing attitudes of African mine workers.

In the larger world, anticolonial feelings were a significant part of international debate. The United Nations became a forum where colonized people could voice their grievances. These trends were magnified by the developing Cold War, during which any regional problem had the potential for becoming an area of contention between the Soviet Union and the United States. Further, the Vatican was quietly encouraging its missionaries to disassociate themselves from colonialism.

Responding to these pressures, the Belgian government began taking steps to improve the status of Africans in the Belgian Congo. In 1952, "worthy Africans" who were able to show that they had reached an adequate "state of civilization," were allowed to fall under the rules of European law, giving them more rights. The next year, the government allowed Africans to own land in rural and urban areas.

Changes were accelerated by the 1954 elections in Belgium. A Socialist-Liberal cabinet took office with an agenda that was

Watusi Herdsman, 1926
By tradition the Watusi are a cattle-raising people. They began to arrive in the Lake Kivu area about 700 years ago, coming from northeastern Africa, probably in search of grazing lands for their herds. Elizabeth Ness photographed this Watusi herdsman with Lake Kivu in the background.

strongly against the Roman Catholic Church. The Trinity that had worked so closely together in the Belgian Congo was beginning to drift apart, and increasing numbers of Africans in the Belgian Congo began talking about independence.

On May 10, 1957, a major reform in local government allowed members of rural councils to be appointed after the preferences of those living in the area were considered. This

Watusi and Twa, 1926 *This Elizabeth Ness photograph contrasts the height of a Watusi (more than seven feet tall) with that of his Twa, or Pygmy, neighbor, who is about five feet. The two groups have had a friendly relationship through the centuries. Today many Pygmies specialize in pottery making, which they market.*

gave Congolese their first taste of democracy since before colonialism. Neighboring French-speaking territories gained independence from their colonial rulers, further fueling people's desire to determine their own future.

Two political groups became the primary voices for the independence movement: The Alliance des Bakongo (ABAKO) and the Congolese National Movement (Mouvement National Congolais; MNC). ABAKO was first formed in 1950 to protect the

Cicatrization, c. 1920 *Cicatrization is the word used to describe the scar formation at the site of a healing wound. In order to create such scar patterns, the skin is lifted with a thorn and cut. Charcoal or ash is then rubbed into the cut to allow the scar tissue to develop without infection. Among the Congolese, these raised scars were tribal marks and usually showed to what tribe a person belonged. Often a more reliable guide than a spoken dialect, the Congolese peoples traditionally used the same tribal scars from generation to generation.*

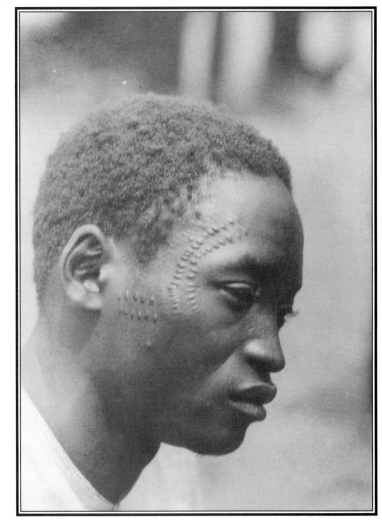

position of the Kongo people. Belgian colonial policy stressed ethnic divisions. They required Congolese to carry identity cards that specified which ethnic group they belonged to. All forms demanded that a person's ethnic group be listed. As Congolese moved to the larger towns, more attention was drawn to the relative economic and social positions that ethnic groups held. In the early 1950s ABAKO wanted to make sure that the Kongo did not lose status to other ethnic groups.

In 1956, however, ABAKO called for immediate self-government. Led by Joseph Kasavubu, a civil servant who had been educated by Roman Catholic missionaries, ABAKO spread anticolonial sentiments and protests throughout the lower Congo and eventually to the rest of the colony. Their goal was independence for the Belgian Congo, with some autonomy for the Kongo region.

In contrast, the MNC started in October 1956 as the first nationwide Congolese political party. It became a force to be reckoned with in 1958 when Patrice Lumumba, a Congolese trade union leader and political activist, became its leader. His outlook was revolutionized in December of the same year when he went to the first All-African People's Conference in Accra, Ghana. There he met people from all over the African continent who were working for national independence. Lumumba returned to the Belgian Congo a militant nationalist.

Less than a month later, on January 4, 1959, a large crowd of ABAKO supporters gathered for a political meeting in Leopoldville. The colonial administrators tried to disperse the group, and anti-European rioting broke out across the city. When order was restored, official reports stated that 49 Congolese were killed and 101 wounded.

The Belgian government wanted to get out of the Congo. It announced a five-year plan leading to independence. The first in a series of local elections would take place in December 1959. Nationalists were skeptical. They wondered if this proposal was simply a Belgian scheme to place Congolese in office who would later follow instructions from Belgium. The MNC announced it would boycott the elections. Belgium responded by repressing political activism. On October 30, 1959, colonial authorities and supporters of independence clashed in Stanleyville. Thirty people died, and Lumumba was thrown in jail on charges of inciting to riot.

The Belgian government decided that its five-year plan was not going to work. It wanted to get out of the Congo immediately. A Round Table Conference was scheduled for January

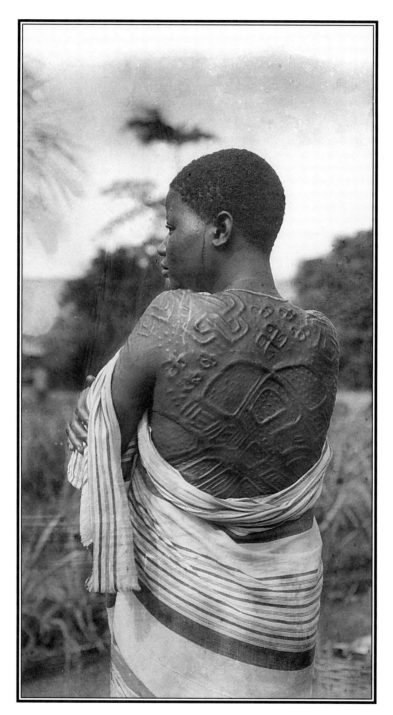

Cicatrization, Central Congo, 1905 Although cicatrization is a form of adornment among many Congo tribes, it is difficult to imagine this woman being willing to endure the pain of these deep cuts, followed by the still more painful process of retarding the healing of the wounds so as to obtain the highly raised scars.

1960 in Brussels. They would gather the numerous Congolese political parties to discuss granting independence as quickly as possible. The MNC refused to participate unless its leader Lumumba attended, so he was released from jail.

The conference agreed to hold national elections in May and declare independence on June 30, 1960. A special commission developed a new constitution for the Congo Republic. It was very similar to the Belgian constitution. A divided executive branch consisted of a president and prime minister. The theory was that the president would act as a figurehead, much like the Belgian king. In practice, it created a major power struggle.

Other problems faced the Congolese. In 1960 the entire Congo contained fewer than 30 Africans with university training. The Force Publique had no Congolese officers. African engineers, doctors, and agricultural experts did not exist. The civil service contained 5,000 management positions, but only three were held by Africans. Belgium was leaving its colony poorly equipped to have a stable government, army, or people.

The May elections brought mixed results. The MNC and ABAKO formed a coalition government, with Patrice Lumumba as the prime minister and Joseph Kasavubu as the president. Lumumba, a powerful public speaker, asserted that true independence for Africa would not be reached until it was no longer an economic colony of Europe.

Western nations were alarmed by Lumumba's language. Belgian, British, and U.S. companies had heavily invested in the Congo because of its natural resources—including copper, cobalt, diamonds, and gold. If the message of the Congo's prime minister took root, these western companies might get kicked out of the country. They were also concerned that Lumumba was turning to the Soviet Union for help.

Then the army mutinied because its Belgian commander refused to give leadership roles to any Congolese. The south-central province of Katanga, bordering Angola and Northern Rhodesia, seceded from the Congo. Belgium immediately sent in troops, allegedly to protect Belgian citizens. In actuality the troops supported the breakaway province.

At the request of the Congo, the United Nations sent troops to restore order. They were unsuccessful. Then Lumumba asked the Soviet Union to provide planes to transport his troops to Katanga. These moves alarmed President Kasavubu, who had leanings toward western powers. He dismissed Lumumba as prime minister on September 5, 1960. Lumumba argued that Kasavubu lacked the legal authority to fire him.

During this power struggle, Congolese Army Colonel Joseph Mobutu seized power. He eventually reached an arrangement with Kasavubu, but Lumumba remained in danger. That December Lumumba was arrested. On January 17, 1961, he was handed over to Katangan authorities and murdered. Years later it was revealed that the U.S. National Security Council subcommittee on covert operations, which included the head of the CIA, had authorized a covert assassination of Lumumba. A CIA operative disposed of the body in an unmarked grave.

Katanga returned to the Congo in 1963. The next year, Kasavubu asked Katanga's leader, Moise Tshombe, to become prime minister. He was needed to quell a rebellion in the eastern provinces. A power struggle developed between Kasavubu and Tshombe. Joseph Mobutu, now commander in chief of the army, once again seized control of the government. He ruled for the next 32 years.

Mobutu's hold on power was tenuous. He relied on U.S. aid to help put down several coup attempts, mostly originating from Katanga forces staying in neighboring Angola. Mobutu curried financial support from Western nations by providing a secure staging area for CIA and French military operations. He stashed away millions of dollars in private accounts and dealt ruthlessly with political enemies.

Wanting to Africanize the name of his country, Mobutu changed it (in 1971) to Zaire, a name based on a mispronunciation of the Portuguese word for the area. He also changed his own name to Mobutu Sese Seko Koko Ngbendu Wa Za Banga ("The all-powerful warrior who, because of his endurance and inflexible will to win, will go from conquest to conquest, leaving fire in his wake").

Belgian Officials at a Gathering of Congo Chiefs, c. 1920 *Throughout the 1920s Belgian Congo administrators decisively supported and encouraged large-scale European economic investments with the promise of cheap and docile laborers—and high profits. As the governor general explained in 1922,*

> *Private initiative is the principal force in the development and economic expansion of the Colony. It must be attracted, assisted, and stimulated; such is the categorical desire of the government, and those who think otherwise run counter to the general interest and are undesirable.*

When independence finally came to the Congo in 1960, in the entire Belgian territory there were fewer than 30 African university graduates. There were no Congolese army officers, engineers, or medical doctors. Of some 5,000 management-level positions in the Belgian Congo civil service force, only three posts were filled by Africans.

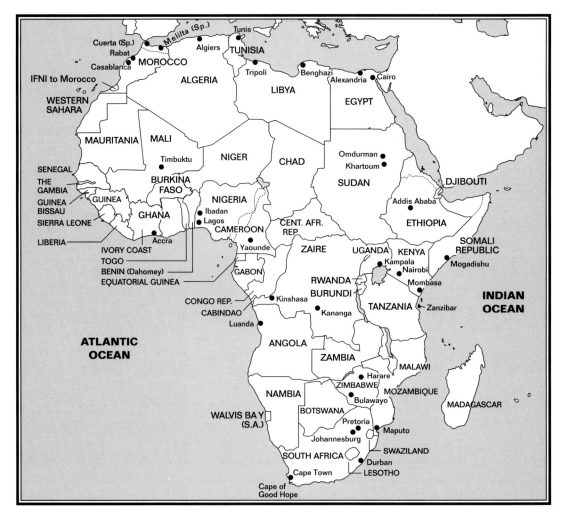

Modern-Day Africa

The end of the Cold War in the 1990s significantly decreased financial support for Zaire from the West, making Mobutu more vulnerable. In April 1990 he lifted the ban on opposition parties, but the next month he put down student protests, resulting in between 50 and 150 students being killed. The next year he relinquished some of his power and in 1994 agreed to government reforms, but the promised elections never took place.

Rebel forces gained strength, and in May 1997, with rebels advancing from the east on the capital Kinshasha (formerly

Leopoldville), Mobutu fled. Rebel leader Laurent Kabila became Zaire's new head of state and quickly changed the name of the country back to the Democratic Republic of the Congo.

Kabila showed a knack for losing friends. He offended South African president Nelson Mandela. He affronted governments that had been anxious to send his country money. He angered the Rwandans, who had helped him overthrow Mobutu.

The Congo quickly became involved in what some call Africa's first world war. Rebels in the eastern provinces of the Congo are backed by Rwanda and Uganda, while Kabila receives support from Angola, Namibia, and Zimbabwe. Conflict centers over ethnic hatred, desire for natural resources, and lust for power. Hundreds of thousands of people have been killed. Nations that during the Cold War had a vested interest in supporting various African governments are now reluctant to spend the resources needed to stabilize the region.

On 18 January 2001, the Congo government confirmed that President Laurent Kabila had been killed. Although the government's announcement gave no details of how he died, most reports have said that he was shot by a bodyguard.

In its announcement, the government also signaled its intention to continue Kabila's 29-month war against rebels supported by Rwanda and Uganda — a war that has thrown all of Central Africa into disorder. These rebel groups immediately called for a renewed commitment to the mid-1999 peace accord that had been negotiated by the United Nations – (though not respected by any side). When informed of Kabila's death, UN Secretary General Kofi Annan stated: "I want to reaffirm the world's determination to play a key role in finding a peaceful solution in the Democratic Republic of Congo." But, four years after Kabila had seized power in the Congo, the question confronting the outside world still remained whether Central Africa is ready for democracy.

The brutal legacy of exploration, terror, and death left behind by King Leopold and others like him has transformed the Congo into a haunted realm. But the traditions of people who lived in the Congo long before Europeans arrived offer a path to a hopeful future rooted in past strengths. The Bambuti are guardians of the wisdom of the earliest human communities and call for a life of simplicity and cooperation, lived in harmony with the natural world. The Kuba developed trade policies that strengthened Africans and preserved artistic and cultural riches. The Kongo designed a uniquely African form of government that draws diverse groups together without crushing them. It remains for the people of the Congo to decide which traditions will lead them into the 21st century.

CHRONOLOGY

1877	On August 12, Henry M. Stanley becomes the first white person to successfully trace the route of the Congo River to its mouth along the western coast of Africa
1878	Stanley first visits Leopold II, king of the Belgians
1879–1884	Under contract to Leopold, Stanley establishes stations along the Congo River and gets hundreds of village chiefs to sign treaties that turn their land and people over to Leopold
1885	Berlin Act is passed, recognizing King Leopold's claims to the Congo basin
1887	Surveying of the railroad around the 220 miles of rapids at the mouth of the Congo River begins
1888	King Leopold establishes the Force Publique, a group of mercenary African soldiers directed by white officers who force other Africans to obey the directives of the colonial authorities and companies
1889	During an anti-slavery conference in Brussels, European powers agree to pay duties in exchange for making use of transportation and support in the Congo as they fight the slave trade in Africa; this nullifies free-trade provisions of the Berlin Act
1890	Joseph Conrad spends six months in the Congo; this experience becomes the basis for his novel *Heart of Darkness;* George Washington Williams' Open Letter is published, attacking Leopold's policies; King Leopold institutes children's colonies in the Congo to provide future soldiers
1892	African-American missionary William Sheppard makes first contact with the Kuba kingdom

CHRONOLOGY

1894	Leopold's forces win brutal war against slave traders in eastern regions of Congo
1895	Congo officer kills a white man, raising European doubts about how Africans are treated; Leopold responds by forming powerless Commission for the Protection of the Natives
1898	Railroad around rapids at mouth of Congo River is completed; ceremony honoring this accomplishment is held at Stanley Pool
1900	Kuba kingdom is overwhelmed by Leopold's forces and its people go into forced labor; E. D. Morel anonymously publishes series of articles about "The Congo Scandal"
1904	Casement Report released, confirming all of Morel's allegations about abuses in the Congo; Congo Reform Association founded; Henry M. Stanley dies
1905	Scathing report of Leopold's Commission of Enquiry released, confirming Morel's and Casement's charges
1906	World consensus that Leopold must give up the Congo
1908	Belgian Congo formed, making the Congo a Belgian colony
1909	King Leopold dies on December 17
1913	Britain recognizes the Belgian Congo; the Congo Reform Association holds its last meeting
1950	Formation of ABAKO to protect the position of Kongo people in the Belgian Congo; becomes a voice for independence
1956	Congolese National Movement founded as first national Congolese political party
1959	On January 4, colony officials try to break up meeting of ABAKO supporters; rioting breaks out and at least 49 Congolese are killed
1960	Round Table Meeting in Brussels lays foundation for Congo independence; elections held in May; Democratic Republic of the Congo established in June
1961	On January 17, prime minister Patrice Lumumba is assassinated
1965	Military coup leads to 32-year rule by commander in chief Joseph Mobutu
1971	Nation's name changed to Zaire
1997	Mobutu driven from office; Laurent Kabila takes control; nation's name changes back to Democratic Republic of the Congo
1998	War involving neighboring nations breaks out; fighting occurs throughout the Congo
2001	Laurent Kabila assassinated by one of his bodyguards; Kabila's son takes control

WORLD WITHOUT END

DEIRDRE SHIELDS

ONE SUMMER'S DAY in 1830, a group of Englishmen met in London and decided to start a learned society to promote "that most important and entertaining branch of knowledge—Geography," and the Royal Geographical Society (RGS) was born.

The society was formed by the Raleigh Travellers' Club, an exclusive dining club, whose members met over exotic meals to swap tales of their travels. Members included Lord Broughton, who had travelled with the poet Byron, and John Barrow, who had worked in the iron foundries of Liverpool before becoming a force in the British Admiralty.

From the start, the Royal Geographical Society led the world in exploration, acting as patron and inspiration for the great expeditions to Africa, the Poles, and the Northwest Passage, that elusive sea connection between the Atlantic and Pacific. In the scramble to map the world, the society embodied the spirit of the age: that English exploration was a form of benign conquest.

The society's gold medal awards for feats of exploration read like a Who's Who of famous explorers, among them David Livingstone, for his 1855 explorations in Africa; the American explorer Robert Peary, for his 1898 discovery of the "northern termination of the Greenland ice"; Captain Robert Scott, the first Englishman to reach the South Pole, in 1912; and on and on.

Today the society's headquarters, housed in a red-brick Victorian lodge in South Kensington, still has the effect of a gentleman's club, with courteous staff, polished wood floors, and fine paintings.

AFTERWORD

The building archives the world's most important collection of private exploration papers, maps, documents, and artefacts. Among the RGS's treasures are the hats Livingstone and Henry Morton Stanley wore at their famous meeting ("Dr. Livingstone, I presume?") at Ujiji in 1871, and the chair the dying Livingstone was carried on during his final days in Zambia. The collection also includes models of expedition ships, paintings, dug-out canoes, polar equipment, and Charles Darwin's pocket sextant.

The library's 500,000 images cover the great moments of exploration. Here is Edmund Hillary's shot of Sherpa Tenzing standing on Everest. Here is Captain Lawrence Oates, who deliberately walked out of his tent in a blizzard to his death because his illness threatened to delay Captain Scott's party. Here, too is the American Museum of Natural History's 1920 expedition across the Gobi Desert in dusty convoy (the first to drive motorised vehicles across a desert).

The day I visited, curator Francis Herbert was trying to find maps for five different groups of adventurers at the same time from the largest private map collection in the world. Among the 900,000 items are maps dating to 1482 and ones showing the geology of the moon and thickness of ice in Antarctica, star atlases, and "secret" topographic maps from the former Soviet Union.

The mountaineer John Hunt pitched a type of base camp in a room at the RGS when he organised the 1953 Everest expedition that put Hillary and Tenzing on top of the world. "The society was my base, and source of my encouragement," said the late Lord Hunt, who noted that the nature of that work is different today from what it was when he was the society's president from 1976 to 1980. "When I was involved, there was still a lot of genuine territorial exploration to be done. Now, virtually every important corner—of the land surface, at any rate—has been discovered, and exploration has become more a matter of detail, filling in the big picture."

The RGS has shifted from filling in blanks on maps to providing a lead for the new kind of exploration, under the banner of geography: "I see exploration not so much as a question of 'what' and 'where' anymore, but 'why' and 'how': How does the earth work, the environment function, and how do we manage our resources sustainably?" says the society's director, Dr. Rita Gardner. "Our role today is to answer such questions at the senior level of scientific research," Gardner continues, "through our big, multidisciplinary expeditions, through the smaller expeditions we support and encourage, and by advancing the subject of geography, advising governments, and encouraging wider public understanding. Geography is the subject of the 21st century because it embraces everything—peoples, cultures, landscapes, environments—and pulls them all together."

The society occupies a unique position in world-class exploration. To be invited to speak at the RGS is still regarded as an accolade, the ultimate seal of approval of Swan, who in 1989 became the first person to walk to both the North and South Poles, and who says, "The hairs still stand on the back of my neck when I think about the first time I spoke at the RGS. It was the greatest honour."

The RGS set Swan on the path of his career as an explorer, assisting him with a 1979 expedition retracing Scott's journey to the South Pole. "I was a Mr. Nobody, trying to raise seven million dollars, and getting nowhere," says Swan. "The RGS didn't tell me I was mad—they gave me access to Scott's private papers. From those, I found fifty sponsors who had supported Scott, and persuaded them to fund me. On the basis of a photograph I found of one of his chaps sitting on a box of 'Shell Spirit,' I got Shell to sponsor the fuel for my ship."

The name "Royal Geographical Society" continues to open doors. Although the society's actual membership—some 12,600 "fellows," as they are called—is small, the organisation offers an incomparable network of people, experience, and expertise. This is seen in the work of the Expeditionary Advisory Centre. The EAC was established in 1980 to provide a focus for would-be explorers. If you want to know how to raise sponsorship, handle snakes safely, or find a mechanic for your trip across the Sahara, the EAC can help. Based in Lord Hunt's old Everest office, the EAC funds some 50 small expeditions a year and offers practical training and advice to hundreds more. Its safety tips range from the pragmatic—"In subzero temperatures, metal spectacle frames can cause frostbite (as can earrings and nose-rings)"—to the unnerving—"Remember: A decapitated snake head can still bite."

The EAC is unique, since it is the only centre in the world that helps small-team, low-budget expeditions, thus keeping the amateur—in the best sense of the word—tradition of exploration alive.

AFTERWORD

"The U.K. still sends out more small expeditions per capita than any other country," says Dr. John Hemming, director of the RGS from 1975 to 1996. During his tenure, Hemming witnessed the growth in exploration-travel. "In the 1960s we'd be dealing with 30 to 40 expeditions a year. By 1997 it was 120, but the quality hadn't gone down—it had gone up. It's a boom time for exploration, and the RGS is right at the heart of it."

While the EAC helps adventure-travellers, it concentrates its funding on scientific field research projects, mostly at the university level. Current projects range from studying the effect of the pet trade on Madagscar's chameleons, to mapping uncharted terrain in the south Ecuadorian cloud forest. Jen Hurst is a typical "graduate" of the EAC. With two fellow Oxford students, she received EAC technical training, support, and a $2,000 grant to do biological surveys in the Kyabobo Range, a new national park in Ghana.

"The RGS's criteria for funding are very strict," says Hurst. "They put you through a real grilling, once you've made your application. They're very tough on safety, and very keen on working alongside people from the host country. The first thing they wanted to be sure of was whether we would involve local students. They're the leaders of good practice in the research field."

When Hurst and her colleagues returned from Ghana in 1994, they presented a case study of their work at an EAC seminar. Their talk prompted a $15,000 award from the BP oil company for them to set up a registered charity, the Kyabobo Conservation Project, to ensure that work in the park continues, and that followup ideas for community-based conservation, social, and education projects are developed. "It's been a great experience, and crucial to the careers we hope to make in environmental work," says Hurst. "And it all started through the RGS."

The RGS is rich in prestige but it is not particularly wealthy in financial terms. Compared to the National Geographic Society in the U.S., the RGS is a pauper. However, bolstered by sponsorship from such companies as British Airways and Discovery Channel Europe, the RGS remains one of Britain's largest organisers of geographical field research overseas.

The ten major projects the society has undertaken over the last 20 or so years have spanned the world, from Pakistan and Oman to Brunei and Australia. The scope is large—hundreds of people are currently working in the field and the emphasis is multidisciplinary, with the aim to break down traditional barriers, not only among the different strands of science but also among nations. This is exploration as The Big Picture, preparing blueprints for governments around the globe to work on. For example, the 1977 Mulu (Sarawak) expedition to Borneo was credited with kick-starting the international concern for tropical rain forests.

The society's three current projects include water and soil erosion studies in Nepal, sustainable land use in Jordan, and a study of the Mascarene Plateau in the western Indian Ocean, to develop ideas on how best to conserve ocean resources in the future.

Projects adhere to a strict code of procedure. "The society works only at the invitation of host governments and in close co-operation with local people," explains Winser. "The findings are published in the host countries first, so they can get the benefit. Ours are long-term projects, looking at processes and trends, adding to the sum of existing knowledge, which is what exploration is about."

Exploration has never been more fashionable in England. More people are travelling adventurously on their own account, and the RGS's increasingly younger membership (the average age has dropped in the last 20 years from over 45 to the early 30s) is exploration-literate and able to make the fine distinctions between adventure / extreme / expedition / scientific travel.

Rebecca Stephens, who in 1993 became the first British woman to summit Everest, says she "pops along on Monday evenings to listen to the lectures." These occasions are sociable, informal affairs, where people find themselves talking to such luminaries as explorer Sir Wilfred Thesiger, who attended Haile Selassie's coronation in Ethiopia in 1930, or David Puttnam, who produced the film *Chariots of Fire* and is a vice president of the RGS. Shortly before his death, Lord Hunt was spotted in deep conversation with the singer George Michael.

Summing up the society's enduring appeal, Shane Winser says, "The Royal Geographical Society is synonymous with exploration, which is seen as something brave and exciting. In a sometimes dull, depressing world, the Royal Geographical Society offers a spirit of adventure people are always attracted to."

FURTHER READING

AFRICA NEWS on the World Wide Web at http://www.africanews.org.

Benedetto, Robert. ed. *Presbyterian Reformers in Central Africa: A Documentary Account of the American Presbyterian Congo Mission and the Human Rights Struggle in the Congo, 1890–1918.* vol. 16 in Studies in Christian Mission. Leiden, The Netherlands: E. J. Brill, 1997.

The Christian Science Monitor archives at http://www.csmonitor.com.

Cline, Catherine Ann. *E. D. Morel: 1873–1924: The Strategies of Protest.* Belfast, Northern Ireland: Blackstaff Press, 1980.

Cocks, F. Seymour. *E. D. Morel: The Man and His Work.* London: George Allen, 1920.

Duffy, Kevin. *Children of the Forest: Africa's Mbuti Pygmies.* Prospect Heights, Ill.: Waveland Press, 1996.

Encyclopedia Britannica Online at http://www.eb.com.

Forbath, Peter. *The River Congo: The discovery, exploration and exploitation of the world's most dramatic river.* New York: Harper & Row, 1977.

Franklin, John Hope. *George Washington Williams: A Biography.* Chicago: Univ. of Chicago, 1985.

Hochschild, Adam. *King Leopold's Ghost.* New York: Houghton Mifflin, 1998.

Pakenham, Thomas. *The Scramble for Africa.* New York: Avon, 1991.

Shaloff, Stanley. *Reform in Leopold's Congo.* Richmond, Va.: John Knox, 1970.

Singleton–Gates, Peter and Maurice Girodias. *The Black Diaries: An account of Roger Casement's life and times with a collection of his diaries and public writings.* New York: Grove Press, 1959.

Stanley, Henry M. *Through the Dark Continent.* vol. 1, 1899 reprinted New York: Dover Publications, 1988.

Turnbull, Colin M. *The Forest People.* New York: Simon & Schuster, 1968.

INDEX

ABOUT THE AUTHORS

Dr. Richard E. Leakey is a distinguished paleo-anthropologist and conservationist. He is chairman of the Wildlife Clubs of Kenya Association and the Foundation for the Research into the Origins of Man. He presented the BBC-TV series *The Making of Mankind* (1981) and wrote the accompanying book. His other publications include *People of the Lake* (1979) and *One Life* (1984). Richard Leakey, along with his famous parents, Louis and Mary, was named by *Time* magazine as one of the greatest minds of the twentieth century.

Bruce and Becky Durost Fish are freelance writers and editors who have worked on more than one hundred books for children and young adults, including *Benjamin Franklin* and *The History of the Democratic Party* in the COLONIAL LEADERS and YOUR GOVERNMENT series respectively.

Deirdre Shields is the author of many articles dealing with contemporary life in Great Britain. Her essays have appeared in *The Times*, *The Daily Telegraph*, *Harpers & Queen*, and *The Field*.